P9-CQK-441

After the Faith Decision

All Else Is Stewardship

After The Faith Decision...

All else is stewardship

Belleville, Ontario, Canada

AFTER THE FAITH DECISION

Copyright © 2007, Lorne W. Jackson

All Rights Reserved. No part of this publication may be reproduced, stored in a retrieval system or transmitted in any form or by any means—electronic, mechanical, photocopy, recording or any other—except for brief quotations in printed reviews, without the prior permission of the author.

Scripture taken from the HOLY BIBLE, NEW INTERNATIONAL VERSION ®. Copyright © 1973, 1978, 1984 by International Bible Society. Used by permission of Zondervan Publishing House. All rights reserved. • Scripture quotations marked NLT are taken from *The Holy Bible,* New Living Translation. Copyright © 1996. Used by permission of Tyndale House Publishers, Inc., Wheaton, IL 60187. All rights reserved. • Scripture quotations marked NKJV are taken from the New King James Version. Copyright © 1979, 1980, 1982. Thomas Nelson Inc., Publishers. • Scripture quotations marked KJV, are from *The Holy Bible, King James Version.* Copyright © 1977, 1984, Thomas Nelson Inc., Publishers.• Scripture taken from *The Message*, copyright © by Eugene H. Peterson, 1993, 1994, 1995. Used by permission of NavPress Publishing Group.

Library and Archives Canada Cataloguing in Publication

Jackson, Lorne W. (Lorne Winston), 1946-

After the faith decision : all else is stewardship / Lorne W. Jackson. ISBN 978-1-55452-167-8 1. Stewardship, Christian. I. Title.

BV772.J32 2007 248'.6 C2007-902314-2

For more information or to order additional copies, please contact:

Canadian National Christian Foundation
300 Earl Grey Drive, suite 435
Ottawa On K2T 1C1
1-866-336-3315 or www.cncf.ca

Guardian Books is an imprint of *Essence Publishing,* a Christian Book Publisher dedicated to furthering the work of Christ through the written word. For more information, contact:

20 Hanna Court, Belleville, Ontario, Canada K8P 5J2
Phone: 1-800-238-6376 • Fax: (613) 962-3055
E-mail: info@essence-publishing.com
Web site: www.essence-publishing.com

Printed in Canada
by

Guardian
BOOKS

Dedication

I would like to dedicate this book to my mom and dad, Warren and Vivian Jackson. My early lessons on stewardship came to me from them as I was raised on a dairy farm about thirty miles south of Ottawa, Ontario, Canada. To this very day they have always been an excellent example of God's love, discipline, and faithfulness. Thank you Mom and Dad; you will never know the value of the example you have set for me all these years. May God give you both many more, healthy and happy years together.

ACKNOWLEDGEMENTS

I HAVE DISCOVERED THAT WHEN YOU AUTHOR A BOOK IT IS never done alone. It is a collaborative effort of many. First I want to thank God for His loving, patient persistent work in my life. He is God, I am not. May I live each day from here forward to serve ONLY Him.

Next I want to thank my mentor and closest friend Larry Brune. Brother, you have truly shown me how Christian brothers should interact with each other and I thank you. Thanks to Gerry Organ, Dave Rae, Mark Peterkins and Kari Yli-Renko for their many years of input into my life. I also want to thank our staff at the Canadian National Christian Foundation, Rick Harper and Greta Luimes, for their help with my work at the foundation and also for the help they gave me in taking the time to read and re-read this book as I was preparing it for publication.

I owe a great deal of gratitude to my long time friend and business associate Jan Kupecz. Jan took on the unenviable task of trying to take my notes and thoughts as I wrote this book and turn them into something that others could actually read and understand. Jan, without you this book would not have been possible.

And last but not least, I want to thank my wife Doris, whom I love very much. She has always been there to support and help me in all my endeavors. Proverbs 31:10-12 "An excellent wife who can find? For her worth is far above jewels. The heart of her husband trusts in her and he will have no lack of gain. She does him good and not evil all the days of her life."

How to Read AND USE THIS BOOK

I KNOW WE ALL LIVE BUSY LIVES AND LIKE MOST, YOU probably have little time for reading and reflection so I thought I would help you to navigate this book. Be sure to read the introduction to the book as it sets the foundation tor why I wrote the book. From there each chapter deals with an aspect of stewardship and reveals lessons I have learned along my life journey. You certainly can jump from chapter to chapter and read each one in isolation if you like, but you will miss the thread of how God has intervened in my life to teach me these lessons.

Throughout the book you will notice that my personal story is interwoven and identifiable by a change in font and indentation. Each of those little vignettes is a glimpse into a time in my life where God used my circumstances to reveal a principle of stewardship to me and how I tried to learn and live accordingly.

At the end of each chapter are "Kingdom Meditations", questions to ponder and possibly use as a devotional to connect with the heart of God and His purposes and guidance for your life.

May God use this to speak courage into your life and bless you as you seek to Serve His Kingdom.

FOREWORD

I HAVE KNOWN LORNE JACKSON FOR ALMOST THIRTY YEARS and have been privileged to see God's handiwork as he has shaped and chiseled away at this man of faith until he could be uniquely useful in the Master's hand. There are many Christians engaged in the business, corporate and financial sectors of our nation, but only when they each come to a place of surrender and brokenness before the Lord, can they be effective ambassadors in their respective areas of giftedness and expertise.

Lorne is striving to become such an ambassador of the gospel in the rigid environment of financial services. As I served for almost ten years as Executive Director of Christian Business Ministries (CBMC), I longed for the day when Christians would be leaders across Canada in providing financial counsel, investment strategies and money management seminars from a biblical point of view. While Crown Financial serves the churches in this area Lorne Jackson is a business leader who is fully qualified and passionately engaged in changing the landscape among financial advisors. This is a tremendous step forward for the industry and for the nation.

The text that Lorne has written is intended to provide penetrating insights into the eternal financial principles imbedded in the pages of scripture. His faith journey and his life story will also touch you personally and spiritually. Lorne and his wife Doris would be thrilled if you discover new truths and receive a measure of God's blessing as you read this book.

> "Heed instruction and be wise; and do not neglect it.
> Blessed is the man who listens to me...
> For he who finds me finds life,
> And obtains favour from the Lord."
>
> (Proverbs 8: 33-35)

Gerry Organ

In 2007 Gerry joined the leadership team at One Way Ministries of Ottawa and will work with the founder and his friend Larry Brune. Gerry will give direction to a national strategy to bring about greater unity to the Body of Christ, His Church, by associating with pastors and marketplace leaders and encouraging them to pursue this objective.

For the past ten years Gerry has served as Executive Director of Christian Business Ministries Canada (CBMC).

Gerry and Lore, his wife of thirty-eight years, live in KIng City, Ontario and are blessed with two married children and five grandchildren.

www.onewayministries.ca

Table of CONTENTS

The Journey 15
Honouring, Obeying, Trusting: A Firm Foundation . . .23
Getting the Right Attitude 35
Enslavement to Debt 47
Contentment: How Much Is Enough? 59
Learning to Trust Him 67
Giving 73
Saving and Investing 81
The Workplace 91
Serving the Kingdom 107
Appendix A: The Faith Decision 115
Appendix B: Helpful Resources 119

The JOURNEY

THIS BOOK IS THE STORY OF MY STEWARDSHIP JOURNEY, A journey that began with some of my earliest life lessons as a child and will end when I leave this life and stand before my heavenly Father, hoping to hear those cherished words *"Well done, good and faithful servant!"* (Matthew 25:21). You will notice that the focus is on God's revelation about my attitude towards and my handling of money. Even though I now understand that stewardship is about more than money, I have chosen to make it a major focus in this book for several reasons.

Firstly, this is the story of how I came to be the president of the Canadian National Christian Foundation (CNCF). CNCF is a ministry organization that amongst other things is dedicated to helping Christians free themselves from the bondage of debt and experience the joy and fulfillment of a generous life. And much of that story has to do with God speaking into my life and my handling of money.

Secondly, God spoke more about money and possessions in the Bible than He did about heaven and hell combined—over 2,350 times. Did you know that sixteen of the thirty-eight parables recorded in the Bible deal with money and possessions? Jesus obviously felt that we needed help and guidance in this area. Could it be because money and possessions are so often used by Satan to distract us from the things that have eternal value?

Let me say right up front that I believe that our handling of money is a very clear and identifiable indicator of the state of our relationship with God—an outward indicator of our inner state. We can fake our talk and fake our walk, we can even fake our Kingdom service, but our cheque book tells its own story about whom we serve. If we cannot be trusted stewards with this most mundane form of treasure, if we are hoarders here on earth, how can we be trusted with those things that truly count for all eternity? So I think that getting our understanding and attitude about money and possessions right is a critical first step.

Back in the 1960s and '70s there was a phrase that was just coming into fashion, *born-again Christian,* and the use of this phrase was certain to get a reaction from people. Initially the reaction might have been one of curiosity, interest even. But as understanding increased, the phrase became synonymous with all things unpleasant about "religious" folk. It's interesting how something that is symbolic of a changed life, a life in submission to the Creator of the universe, came to be so offensive to so many.

I wonder if *stewardship* is another such term. Its true meaning evokes an understanding of who God is and who we are in relation to Him—Creator and creature; master and servant; father and child; lover and beloved. Sadly, amongst many Christians today, *stewardship* has come to mean the annual "money drive" for the church or that "outdated tithing thing." And upon hearing the word, many actually feel offended. "Oh no, here they go again, wanting more of my hard-earned money."

So let me begin with a bold statement that best summarizes my understanding about God's call to His people as His stewards: *After the faith decision, **all else** is stewardship.* I cannot take credit for that statement, and I don't know who rightly should be credited, but it certainly is powerful. And if it is true, then stewardship is about more than money—much more.

To really understand this statement, we need to take it apart. First, let's look at this "faith decision." The faith decision is that very personal and conscious thought you and I had when the Spirit of God invited us into a personal relationship with the one, true, living God through the atoning work of His Son Jesus.[1] And in that moment of revelation, with the prompting of the Spirit, we began to leave behind our little selfish kingdom to enter into the Kingdom of God—a kingdom characterized by a new way of living according to a holy standard set by the Creator of the universe. We consciously said, "Yes, Lord, I will serve you and your Kingdom." We became believers—Christians.

Whether that revelation of Jesus' atoning work was a new revelation for you at a significant moment in your life or a fresh revelation after years of belief and faithfulness, the sense of the presence of God and His Holy Spirit was powerful, and you were passionate in your commitment to serving Him. You wanted to know His plans for you. You wanted to know Him more. You wanted to experience Him more deeply, and above all you desired to be close to Him. You understood that the things of God were not the same as the things of this world. God had a plan for you and for your place in His Kingdom, and you earnestly sought His will for your life.

Does some or all of this resonate with you? Maybe for some of you the passion has waned a bit over time and has been replaced by a rock steady faith in God and a trust in His faithfulness. For others, the passion is as real today as it was at that moment of decision. And for still others, like me, God has always been very real in your life, and rarely can you recall a time when you did not trust in His ways.

---

[1] See Appendix A for a deeper understanding of the Faith Decision.

Whatever the journey has been, this I know to be true for most of us: with God's help we have consciously changed many things in our lives. We have shared the good news of the gospel with many; we have ministered in our local churches and communities; we have repaired broken relationships; we have sought godly counsel in our life choices; we have turned from harshness to display the fruit of the Spirit; we have changed our behaviour and softened our words; we have joined study groups to learn more about Him; we have disciplined our appetites; we have continued to move from selfishness to service, seeking to obey God and therefore to manifest our love for Him. The "faith decision" has changed the way we view the world and the way we live.

Now let's look at the common definition of *stewardship*. The dictionary definition is "the careful and responsible management of something entrusted to one's care." The dictionary also lists *servant* as a synonym for *steward*.

So follow along with me. In seeking to love and obey our Lord, we intentionally alter our lives and our actions. We seek out God's will for us, and we continually reorder our lives to conform to His standards. We seek not only to serve Him but to make Him the Lord of our lives—the one whose commands we seek to follow. And as we make Him Lord, we become His servants. We begin to understand that God has entrusted us with His truth and His gospel. *He has given us care over people, our families and our friends—care that fits with His Kingdom purposes.* He asks us to manage our tongues and our appetites (desires and passions) in order to serve Him better.

So, do you see it? After the faith decision, it really is all about stewardship. In seeking to serve God's kingdom, we become His servants, His stewards—stewards of His truth, stewards of His Word, stewards of our lives, stewards of our service, stewards of our relationships, stewards of our bodies, and stewards of His creation. From the moment we willingly entered through that narrow gate[2] and answered His call to a life of service in His Kingdom, we began a journey of stewardship. We have become managers in the Kingdom. God has entrusted us with the care of His creation and His plan, and He intends to entrust us with much more for all eternity. We should be rejoicing in our role as His stewards.

So why don't we rejoice when we hear teaching about stewardship? For some of us, it may be that our churches have made the discussion of stewardship unpleasant, characterized by threats and guilt. For others it may be a lack of understanding or even fear—fear that in giving more, we may find ourselves without enough of something we need. And for still others it may be a Spirit-induced conviction that we are not walking as we should, and we know it and so rebel at any discussion about stewardship. Whatever the reason, it is time to fully answer and embrace His call to stewardship. Our Lord is returning soon, and we *will* be held accountable. His Word says:

> *Be dressed ready for service and keep your lamps burning, like men waiting for their master to return from a wedding banquet, so that when he comes and knocks they can immediately open the door for him. It will be good for those servants whose master finds them watching when he comes. I tell you the truth, he will dress himself to serve, will have them recline at the table and will come and wait on them. It will be good for those servants whose master finds them ready, even if he comes in the second or third watch of the night* (Luke 12:35–38).

Learning to be a faithful steward for some may mean learning a system of handling money, but for many of us it is about dismantling that final wall in the kingdom of self. If we have truly entered into God's Kingdom and want to serve

[2] Matthew 7:13–14.

Him, now and forever, then the issue is not whose money it is. That question has been answered—*It's all His.*[3] Now the question becomes "What would You have me do with Your money, Lord?" Generosity should be easy for a servant of the Kingdom of God—it's not our money. Jan David Hettinga captures this beautifully in his book *Follow Me:*

> One of the more significant signs of God's activity can be seen when He turns selfishness into generosity. Turning water into wine is child's play when compared to changing the hearts of human beings with regard to money and possessions. Religious people give to create an impression with others and leverage with God. Jesus deliberately exposed the inferior motivation behind the giving of the Pharisees and religious authorities of His day (Matthew 6:1–4).Kingdom people give because they're no longer building their private kingdoms. Part of their worship involves continually transferring ownership of all that they have to their master. The more you see that it really is God's kingdom you're building in hearts, and not man's kingdom, the more your values change. Jesus applauds the practice of "selling all that you have" in order to possess the pearl of great price (see Matthew 13:45–46). It makes no sense to hoard and accumulate for time

[3] Psalm 24:1; 1 Chronicles 29:11–12,14,16.

> what you can give away and keep for eternity. When the kingdom is the focus of a believer's value system, the hold of wealth and possessions radically diminishes.[4]

Horace Bushnell said, "One more revival—only one more—is needed, the revival of Christian stewardship, the consecration of the money power to God. When that revival comes, the Kingdom of God will come in a day."[5] What a wonderful day that will be.

Come with me now as I share my journey with you—my story of how God has dealt with and continues to deal with my little kingdom of self and has helped me to begin to dismantle walls so that I might experience the joy of being a generous giver and live a life that I hope will be pleasing to my Lord and Master.

---

[4] Jan David Hettinga, *Follow Me* (Colorado Springs, Colorado: NavPress, 1996).

[5] Randy Alcorn, *Money, Possessions and Eternity* (Tyndale House Publishers, 2003).

Honouring, Obeying, Trusting: A FIRM FOUNDATION

I TRULY AM BLESSED. I HAVE A WONDERFUL, GODLY Christian heritage that has shaped my life. I can't remember a time when I didn't believe in God and understand that this was His world and I belonged to Him. At age eight, during an evangelistic service, I went forward and accepted Christ as my Saviour. Since that time, I have been working to make Him My Lord as well. And I know that God has been working to teach me lessons so that I can truly serve His purposes here on earth. And I haven't always been the easiest student to teach.

I grew up on a dairy farm, and the first earnings that I can recall came from helping to bring in the hay. I received $1 a day. Dad was not only my first employer but was also my first teacher. He said that when I got paid each weekend I needed to take sixty cents from the $6 that I would make that week and give it to our church. He explained that I should always honour the Lord with a tithe—which he said was 10 percent of whatever I made.

Knowing the heart of a young boy, my dad went on to tell me that when he was young he too felt reluctant to give that 10 percent to God's work. But he did give, and every time he did God would honour that giving, and he would then get more money back than he ever expected.

From then on I always gave 10 percent of my earnings to God's work. When a paycheque arrived, I would write the

> deposit in my cheque book and immediately follow that entry with a 10 percent tithe to my church. Even though I had not yet written the cheque, my bank book showed it as being withdrawn. So when Sunday morning came around, I was always excited to write the cheque—it did not feel like I was giving up anything, because in my mind it was already gone.
>
> But my early learning about giving did not end with these lessons on the tithe of my earnings. My dad seemed to understand the power of giving, and it was woven into our lives in many different ways. In those days on the farm, we didn't have a lot of money, and what we did have went back into the farm to grow more crops and cattle. Every year my dad would kill a cow for our personal consumption and then give one-quarter of it to our pastor. He said that it was his way of tithing on that. I knew that we didn't have as much money as others who could buy their meat at the butcher shop, and yet we gave away 25 percent of what we produced that was supposed to feed our family. What a powerful lesson about honouring God with "firstfruits" (Exodus 23:19).

I may not have fully understood and appreciated the theological implications of those early lessons, but I clearly understood the importance of putting God first. It was modelled for me. Before all else, we looked to God.

As a child, I learned obedience to my earthly father and mother, and I also learned obedience to my heavenly Father. In childlike fashion, I obeyed according to my level of understanding. The older I got, the more I understood and appreciated God's call to obedience. And the more I obeyed and experienced God's blessing, the more I came to trust Him. And the more I trusted Him and involved Him in my life, the more I wanted to honour Him in everything I did. Somewhere along the journey, I came to an understanding that it was a lifelong process to make my Saviour the Lord of my life.

Being raised on the farm, I learned a lot about planting and harvesting. Sometimes we would have some old oats that had been in the granary for a few years. Those oats became very dry inside and very light in weight. If you plant these kinds of seeds, not much will happen. In fact much of the seed will yield nothing, and the rest will produce little of any use. On the farm, if we hoped to reap a good harvest of oats, we had to plant the best seeds. I am reminded of this principle in God's Word when He talks about giving of our "best" or "firstfruits" to His Kingdom. If we hope to harvest a good life, we need to give God our best. For me, this is what it looks like:

> **Time:** I am a morning person. I love to get up early and enjoy the sunrise—unlike some who believe that if God intended us to enjoy a sunrise, He would have made it happen later in the day. If I am truly going to give God my best in the area of my time, that needs to happen early in the day. I am of little use to Him or anyone after 9 p.m. Therefore I commit to spending time with God—my devotion time—first thing in the morning. I want to give God the "firstfruit" of my time. I like to get a cup of coffee and sit down with my Bible, my notebook, and a devotional book by Ken Boa called *Handbook to Prayer*. I always like to start with about ten minutes of worship music and focus on who God is. I then spend the next fifty minutes just praying and listening to my Creator. After five years of doing this, I find I don't like to let anything mess it up. I really look forward to this time alone with God. Did I always enjoy it? No. At first I had to discipline myself to be consistent. I started with a thirty-minute time slot and eventually moved it up to one hour.
>
> **Talent:** God has gifted me in some areas and not in others. For example, I am not gifted in analyzing data or calculating financial statements. I can do it, but it's neither a strength nor a spiri-

tual gift for me. Ironically, most corporate or charity boards I have been on have wanted me on the audit committee or the finance committee. I suppose that's because they thought, "He's a financial planner, so he must be gifted in finance." Wrong. The fund managers and the insurance actuaries did the bulk of that work. My job as a financial planner was a people job. I love being with people. In addition to a spiritual gift of giving, I believe God has given me a talent in working with people. He has also gifted me in the area of helping—coming alongside, giving advice, and helping people work together (being a peacemaker).

I try to prioritize my day so that God gets my best in these areas. Otherwise I might rush through the day doing all kinds of good things but miss God's best for that day. My agenda can be easily derailed by what I think is good for me, not what is best for Him. At the end of the day, I might remember to "tack on" a few gifts of my talents for God—my leftovers, you might say. Not good. He wants my "firstfruits," not my "last leftovers."

Treasure: I also believe that God wants the first of my return on my labour. And I think the principle is the same here—if I sow sparingly or give of my poorest, then that's what I reap. Remember the story in Genesis of Cain and Abel. They were the early descendants of Adam and Eve. Cain became a farmer of the soil and grew crops, whereas Abel became a keeper of flocks. The Bible says,

In the course of time Cain brought some of the fruits of the soil as an offering to the LORD. But Abel brought fat portions from some of the firstborn of his flock. The

> *LORD looked with favor on Abel and his offering, but on Cain and his offering he did not look with favor.*[6]

Notice that the only difference we see in these two men is the fact that *"Abel brought fat portions from some of the firstborn of his flock."* Abel gave the best he had, whereas Cain brought what was left over. The difference wasn't as much about the gift as the attitude with which it was given. Cain gave out of obligation; Abel gave out of joy and a thankful heart.

If God is really my Lord and Master, then I want to give my best as soon as I can. And for me in the area of finances, that means I give 10 percent minimum *before* I pay the mortgage, groceries, rent, etc. If I wait and pay the others first, then I am the same as Cain. I am just giving *some* of my earnings.

"Imagine having God over to a big dinner party but serving His plate last. Oops! The food runs out right before it gets to Him, so you go to the refrigerator and scrape together some leftovers. We would never do that to God. And we shouldn't do it with our finances either. Set aside His portion first, and we won't dishonour our most important guest."[7]

> In the mid 1970s I found myself unemployed for a three-month period. During that time I applied for and received employment insurance benefits from the government. The EI cheque at that time consisted of $210 every two weeks. As my wife, Doris, and I considered this small deposit to our bank account, we realized that this would not cover our monthly needs. However, we determined that tithing was important to us and decided to tithe 10 percent of our cheque. We went through that three-month period and never missed a bill payment, and even though we received no real paycheque for three months plus another month on my new job, we had no outstanding bills. It seemed that nine-tenths could go farther

---

[6] Genesis 4:3–5.

[7] Andy Stanley, *Fields of Gold* (Wheaton, Illinois: Tyndale House Publishers, 2004) pg. 88.

> than ten-tenths. Although this did not make a lot of sense and certainly did not add up mathematically, it was a wonderful lesson about God's care and provision.

Second Corinthians 9:6–11 says if we sow sparingly we will reap sparingly, and if we sow generously we will reap generously. There have been times when I thought I couldn't afford to tithe and would try to bargain with God for something less than 10 percent. I was sowing sparingly. Can you guess how I reaped? I would say, "I can't afford it right now, Lord, but I'll give it later when I have more to give." I never had more to give until *I gave more.* It's like a farmer saying, "I can't afford to put these last few seeds in the ground until I get a better crop." The thing is, if he keeps those seeds in the granary, there *is* no crop. I have found the same with my giving. Generous givers can testify to this principle.

Now I want to be sure that some of you reading this don't jump to the conclusion that I am implying that tithing is a requirement for Christians. That is Old Testament living and perhaps even "legalistic." God's Word says that *"If anyone is in Christ...the old has gone, the new has come."*[8] The old kingdom of self is gone; the new servant of God's Kingdom is here. Jesus Himself did not require tithing that we know of, but He did recommend it in Matthew 23:23. Even while recommending it, He emphasized that it was even more important that we not lose focus on the greater things.

Unfortunately many of us misunderstand the spiritual freedom we have in Christ. Serving God does not restrict our lives; it releases us. I have heard it said that "Freedom is not the right to do what we want but the power to do what we ought." The Law of the Old Testament has indeed been replaced by the Law of Liberty. However, I believe that our attitude towards money indicates how much the gospel has changed us. Of the tithe, author Larry Burkett says, "It is a

---

[8] 2 Corinthians 5:17.

material testimony. It is an outside, visible material indication of an inside spiritual condition. Tithing is not a step in getting closer to God. It is a *result* of getting close to God."[9]

When asked what the greatest commandment was, Jesus replied, *"'Love the Lord your God with all your heart and with all your soul and with all your mind and with all your strength.' The second is this: 'Love your neighbor as yourself.'"*[10] That pretty well covers it all, doesn't it? Can you feel the action in this command of Jesus to love? Unlike our modern-day use of the word *love,* which is more about feelings, the word as it is used here is full of action. When we show love to others, we do things for them. So I am commanded to act out my love for God with all my heart (my centre of passion), all my soul (my centre of being), all my mind (my centre of thinking and reasoning), and all my strength (my actions following out of my thinking). I love the way Eugene Peterson renders it in *The Message, "Love the Lord God with all your passion and prayer and intelligence and energy."*[11]

Now why is it that so often we find ourselves wholeheartedly agreeing with this command but, in the area of serving God with our money and material wealth, we somehow can rationalize that this command is not applicable—that we don't need to serve (love) Him there also?

Have you been in a situation where you had to make an important financial decision, seeking God's input, only to have Him appear disinterested or on vacation? I have. And I finally figured out that this usually occurred immediately following some other financial decision I made where I left God out. I did not invite His input, because I already knew what I wanted to do and I didn't want God to "mess up" my plan. But of course, later when I got into trouble, I wanted His input—

---

[9] Larry Burkett, *Business by the Book* (Nashville, Tennessee: Thomas Nelson Publishers, 1998).

[10] Mark 12:30–31.

[11] Mark 12:30–31 (The Message).

too late. Did I really think God wasn't interested, or was I just rationalizing my disobedience?

I have found that when I hold back any part of my life from God, He respects my wishes and backs out. Some theologians would call that "God withholding His restraining grace." You know that expression we so often use, "There, but for the grace of God, go I." Well, that's the principle. Friends, God is interested in a relationship with us, one founded on love of the highest order. It must pain Him to see our continual attempts to reframe that relationship according to our selfish interests.

Here is where obedience comes into the picture for me. Part of my journey in living out His commands involves overcoming my desire to "feel" before I "act." I never started out "feeling" like loving God with my finances. First I had to act in obedience, and when I did so, the feelings then came. In other words, I needed to give my finances and decisions over to God even when I didn't feel like it or see the need for it. And eventually that obedience changed my feelings, and they fell into line.

Now here's the truth for me—when I am obedient to God, I hear His voice more clearly, I sense His love and caring more consistently, and I find myself wanting to serve Him more fully. I believe that tithing should not be a legalistic requirement to achieve closeness to God; for the Spirit-filled follower of Jesus, it is an indicator of a changing life, one that is prepared to submit all to the One who created all.

If I believe that I am a child of the living God, a servant in the Kingdom of Heaven, and a redeemed sinner destined to be part of the Bride of Christ and reign with Him for all eternity, why would I still be holding on to the idea that in the area of my finances I know better than He does? When I act that way I am saying, "Lord, come into my life and remake me into Your image—but thanks, I'll make the money decisions myself."

Randy Alcorn puts it this way:

When I grasp that I am a steward—not an owner, it totally changes my perspective. Suddenly, I'm not asking, "How much of my money shall I, out of the goodness of my heart, give to God?" Rather, I'm asking, "Since all of 'my' money is really yours, Lord, how would you like me to invest your money today?"[12]

Or think of it the way pastor and author Andy Stanley does:

> Picture yourself receiving ten $1 bills from God. Remember, God is the owner and you're a steward, not an owner. As you look at the bills in your hand, you say, "God, You're handing me ten of Your dollars. What do You want me to do with them? Are You going to want them back?"
> God says, "I just want one of them back."
> Puzzled, you reply, "Just one? Are you sure?"
> "Yep, just give Me one," He says.
> "Well, what do You want me to do with the other nine?" you inquire.
> "Whatever you want," He replies.
> "You mean You're giving me $10, and You want only one back—and I get to keep the other nine for me?" you explain in disbelief.
> You get the idea. Can you imagine hiring a money manager to steward your 401(k)[13] and telling him he can keep 90 percent of it? That's basically what God does with you. If you think about it, all God asks for His investment is a

---

[12] Randy Alcorn, *Money, Possessions and Eternity* (Tyndale House Publishers, revised and updated 2003).

[13] This would be the equivalent of the RRSP in Canada.

> tenth of the principal. It's almost laughable. And to think we struggle to give Him any of it.
>
> If you truly approach your finances as if God were the owner of it all, giving a percentage back to Him is only appropriate. And if you're searching the Bible for a percentage that you can be sure is pleasing to Him—whether you want to call it obedience or just cheerful giving—10 percent is a good place to start (see Genesis 28:22). It was the amount observed in the Old Testament, so there's something about that amount that God has decided is appropriate. Maybe He knows some elaborate formula and 10 percent is the precise amount that will keep our hearts from drifting as our wealth fluctuates.[14]

I have certainly found that God's plan to ensure that my heart is truly all His is the tithe—the 10 percent of my income—as a start.

May I lovingly suggest that if you find yourself arguing against tithing, ask God to reveal to you what is at the heart of your argument. Is there something in your past or in your current reality that is instilling fear in your heart about your financial foundation? Do you trust God with all of your life? Are your feelings about giving to the "church" built upon others' perceptions and attitudes or built upon your own personal relationship with God? Sincerely ask God to reveal the source of your thoughts and attitudes and to replace any faulty thinking with His divine perspective. Can there be anything better than living life with a perspective that honours God and is built upon a foundation of obedience and trust towards the Creator of the universe?

---

[14] Andy Stanley, *Fields of Gold* (Tyndale House Publishers, Wheaton, Illinois, 2004).

Kingdom Meditations

• What early influences in your life shaped your attitude towards God?

• List the things in your life today that honour God.

• Are there things in your life that you think may dishonour God?

• Make a plan of action to bring into alignment those things that dishonour God.

• Reflect on the freedom you have in Christ.

• Make a list of all those things in your life that have changed because of the gospel and the presence of the Holy Spirit in your life.

• Ask God how much He thinks you should be giving. Write down the amount and make it your goal. Periodically revisit how you are doing.

• Have there been times in your life that you have locked God out of decision-making? What was the effect, and what did you learn?

Getting the Right ATTITUDE

A FEW YEARS AGO A BUDDY AND I DECIDED TO LEAD A Sunday morning small group study examining money and possessions and what God's Word has to say about it. We chose a book written by Larry Burkett. I don't remember the name of the book, but I do remember this one thing: *When it comes to money and possessions in our life, it's all about attitude.* The Bible says we can't serve both God and money (Matthew 6:24). However I have learned that we can serve God with money. Over the years, I have also learned that I cannot out-give God. I have found that as I increase my percentage of giving, my net worth also increases.

Second Corinthians 9:7 says, *"Each man should give what he has decided in his heart to give"* (NIV), for *"God loves it when the giver delights in the giving"* (*The Message*). Why does God want me to give? Does He need my money, my time, my talent? Acts 17:25 says, *"He is not served by human hands, as if he needed anything, because he himself gives all men life and breath and everything else."* It is He who gives me the natural talents and abilities to earn an income. So since God does not need my gifts and my giving, why then would He love it when a giver gives from the heart? I believe that He asks me to give because He knows I need it. I need it in order to develop a generous and loving heart. When I give, I am becoming more like Him.

God asks me to give because it helps Him accomplish His work *in me*. Ken Boa says, "As you become a person of calling and purpose, you come to realize that God's good pleasure is also your good pleasure."[15] We should delight in giving—God loves it!

I have heard it said, "To reject God outright is one thing, but to acknowledge Him and then live as if He is neither Lord nor God is a horrible existence." Author Roger Palms says, "We were put on earth by God at this time and this place not for personal gain or personal pleasure but for His purpose."[16]

So you've probably figured out by now that for me tithing is a non-negotiable—in fact, for me, it is just the beginning, the absolute minimum. I learned the lessons early in life, and God has affirmed my faithfulness in a variety of ways. I do not give out of a legalistic requirement to do so but because of my relationship with God. When I consider all that He's done for me, how could I not give? His guidance and faithfulness have shaped my life and blessed me in so many ways.

But I sometimes wonder if the traditional "stewardship-tithe" message that says we should give God one-tenth of our income (treasure) and one-seventh of our week (time and talent) is actually misleading us. Let me explain. I believe that this teaching suggests that we should give a small portion of our produce or income to God and that the rest belongs to us to do with as we please. And God does give us that choice—will we look to Him or to our own pleasures? What this traditional "stewardship sermon" oftentimes fails to fully teach is the truth that God owns it all and we are called to steward it for Him and for His purposes. Unless we understand this truth, any giving we do will not be from the heart but will be done reluctantly and under compulsion. Andy Stanley says, "God knows that someone who gives reluctantly is still thinking like

---

[15] Kenneth Boa, *Conformed to His Image* (Zondervan, 2001).

[16] Roger C. Palms, *Enjoying the Closeness of God* (World Wide Pubs (1989)).

an owner, not a steward. Giving under a sense of compulsion is typically a gift given from leftovers."[17]

Somehow, even in the teaching coming from our pulpits, we manage to communicate that giving to the Lord is painful but necessary. Some years back, while travelling, I attended a church in another city. The pastor got up and said, "Well, folks, today we are going to talk about money. I know you didn't come to church to hear about money, and I don't really want to talk about it either, but we need to." Wow. What a way to back into a teaching that should be uplifting, freeing, and exciting. I believe we can slip into a bad attitude about giving if we think that money is evil or that dealing with it in the church is a "necessary evil." Scripture clearly teaches that it *all* belongs to God. We are His servants, His stewards, whom He has chosen to trust with the care of His creation. What an awesome responsibility and what a tremendous opportunity for us to demonstrate our love and gratitude towards Him!

In the book *Splitting Heirs,* Ron Blue ponders the following question: "What are the implications of God owning it?" He suggests three implications.

1. God can take whatever He wants whenever He wants.
2. Every spending decision is an eternal decision.
3. Stewardship cannot be faked.[18]

1. God can take whatever He wants whenever He wants.

"The LORD gave and the LORD has taken away; may the name of the LORD be praised" (Job 1:21). Ron says, "When you close your hand and say, 'God, you no longer have the right to take your resources,' you have crossed the line from stewardship (responsibilities) into ownership (rights)."

---

[17] Andy Stanley, *Fields of Gold,* (Tyndale House Publishers, revised and updated, 2003).

[18] Ron Blue and Jeremy White, *Splitting Heirs* (Northfield Publishing, 2004).

2. **Every spending decision is an eternal decision.**

If all you have belongs to God, then how you use it affects His purpose for your life. That statement is important enough to read over again—*how you use it affects His purpose for your life.* Wow. Have you ever considered that every spending decision has an impact on God's plans for you here on earth? I wonder if that is the principle behind laying up treasure in heaven (Matthew 6:19–21)—blessing others not only blesses me in the here and now but for eternity, because I am fulfilling God's purpose for my life.

3. **Stewardship cannot be faked.**

Your cheque book tells how you choose to use God's resources. It reveals your priorities—how much debt you have, what your savings and investment philosophy is. Your Daytimer (schedule) also reveals priorities—how you manage your time; what priority you give God, family, and friends. I often wonder, if God asked me today to show Him my cheque book or schedule, would I be happy with what I have to show? More importantly—would He be happy?

With respect to the principle that *God owns it all,* I confess that it is much easier to say and write this than it is to live this out on a daily basis. Psalm 24:1 says, *"The earth is the LORD'S, and all it contains, The world, and those who dwell in it"* (NASB). I can easily get a "head knowledge" that, yes, in fact, God does own it all and that He can do as He chooses with me and around me. But I find it very difficult to truly make this the attitude of my heart and the actions of my will. My friend Ron Blue has again helped me here, he says that;

> I can evaluate the extent to which I have fully surrendered ownership of my life to God by:

- The extent to which I worry about things.
- The extent to which I try to control life.
- The level of my contentment."[19]

These thoughts are certainly worthy of meditation, and I encourage you to consider doing just that and honestly seek God's help to evaluate where you are in surrendering ownership of your life to Him. And if you are anything like me, you will have to do this again and again as the Holy Spirit helps you to sift and sort.

In a subsequent chapter I will share more about contentment, because I believe that this is a critical element for living the truly Spirit-led, abundant life that God desires for us. But in the context of getting the right attitude about money, it has been said that wealth begins with contentment and continues with increase. *Wealth* by definition means having more than enough to pay the bills. If you are unable to live beneath your income, then it's possible to earn millions of dollars and still want more. That's not wealth; that's foolishness and, for some, outright greed. We can never be wealthy no matter how much money we have if we're not content.

Contentment and greed are conditions of the heart. One of these conditions concerning money is present in every human being, Christians included. Just look at what the Word says: *"You ask and do not receive, because you ask amiss, that you may spend it [money] on your pleasures."*[20] *"Lust for money brings trouble and nothing but trouble."*[21] *"But godliness with contentment is great gain."*[22] I have learned that there is a vast difference between a healthy interest in financial things and being driven by or obsessed with money and things. To me the difference between

---

[19] Rob Blue and Jeremy White, *Splitting Heirs,* (Northfield Publishing, 2004).

[20] James 4:3 (NKJV).

[21] 1 Timothy 6:9–11 (The Message).

[22] 1 Timothy 6:6.

being content and being driven is this: When I am driven I keep raising the bar, financial or otherwise, and am never satisfied. It is akin to running a race with no set finish line.

I believe that the contented Christian is one who will make good on opportunities to increase wealth without compromising his or her love for God and people. Contentment is not achieved by unceasingly striving to achieve wealth.

So here are two keys I have learned that help me to align my attitude with God's purpose for my life:

1. Honour God with my wealth. That means that every financial decision is a spiritual decision.
2. Honour Him with the first and best, not what's left over at the end of the month. This is why I think tithing has worked so well for me. It forces me to give it first, and I know where to start. It gives me a guide to use for honouring Him.

And God knows me. He even wants what is best for me! I can trust that *nothing* happens to me that is a surprise to God. Stop and think about that for a moment. Nothing. God is never surprised by my reactions or by the things that are coming at me. He has known it all from before I was born. Psalm 139:1–6 says,

> *O LORD, you have examined my heart and know everything about me. You know when I sit down or stand up. You know my every thought when far away. You chart the path ahead of me and tell me where to stop and rest. Every moment you know where I am. You know what I am going to say even before is say it, LORD. You both precede and follow me. You place your hand of blessing on my head. Such knowledge is too wonderful for me, too great for me to know!* (NLT).

So how can I not trust a God like that? If I give Him Lordship over all areas of my life, it will always work out for my good. He promised. At the time I am not always convinced of this, but I have discovered that when I get to the other side of the event and look back, I can see God's hand all along the way.

And even at this stage in my life, God is teaching me new truths about giving. In 2 Corinthians 9:7 Paul says, *"Each one must do just as he has purposed in his heart, not grudgingly or under compulsion, for God loves a cheerful giver"* (NASB). I am beginning to understand that *how* I give may be more important than *what* I give.

> **Thoughtfully**—not from impulse. My wife, Doris, and I now plan out thoughtfully our giving goals for the year and how much we plan to give to each cause. As an example, we like to plan how much to give to our church (which I think should be 10 percent of my salary—then if I get a bonus or any additional income I can give it outside the church), how much to the poor, to evangelism and other God-driven interests.
>
> **Voluntarily**—not under pressure. I have been to "fundraising" dinners where the pressure to give was pretty intense. I have decided that if I have not had an opportunity to pray and talk to my wife about it ahead of time, I won't give at an event. I do not think that it's God's will that I act out of guilt or human pressure.
>
> **Worshipfully**—as giving is part of our worship of the Creator. As I said earlier, I have observed that many pastors do not like to talk about money and in fact often apologize when bringing it up. Giving is an act of worship, so why should it not be a vital and visible part of our corporate worship gatherings? He has

> shown me that He is trustworthy and worthy of *all* my worship, and that includes money.

I have also found that giving money away helps diffuse the natural temptation to lust for money. It takes the power money might have over me and allows me to focus on others. I believe that Jesus knew this, and that's why He talked so much about money and possessions when He was here on earth. Of the recorded words of Jesus, 15 percent are on this subject.

In Matthew 6:21 the Lord says, *"Where your treasure is, there your heart will be also." The Message* renders it this way: *"It's obvious, isn't it? The place where your treasure is, is the place you will most want to be, and end up being."* Most Bible commentaries will tell us that Jesus is exhorting us not to value possessions enough to seek them. Notice that it doesn't say that what we set our hearts on will become our treasure. No, it says that what we treasure will lead our hearts. As an illustration, let's suppose I use a major portion of my retirement fund to buy Microsoft stock. If I happen to see a news headline that reads "Changes at Microsoft have a Big Effect on Shareholders," I probably am a lot more interested than I was before I owned their stock. So my heart is seeking to know more about where I already put my treasure.

What we treasure might not always be money. You may be quite willing to give money freely but treasure your time. Then you may need to examine where you give your time. How much time do you give to charitable causes and Kingdom work? If you seek to have a heart for God's work, then you need to be prepared to put your most prized possessions there.

The bottom line with respect to our attitude is best summed up by Randy Alcorn, who says, "Stewardship is not a subcategory of the Christian life. Stewardship *is* the Christian life."[23]

---

[23] Randy Alcorn, *Money, Possessions and Eternity* (Tyndale House Publishers, revised and updated, 2003).

In 1977, after three months of unemployment and no job prospects, I decided to train as a life insurance salesman. I felt at that point that God did not intend me to do that for very long. I was pretty sure that I would not like the financial industry. However, I reluctantly agreed to go into insurance sales, figuring that I would learn whatever God wanted me to learn and then I would go on to a "real" job. You see, even though I didn't want to be in the insurance business, I did believe that God's plans were always for my good. I guess I must be a slow learner, because I spent twenty-five years in the financial services business before I heard God's current call for my life. Starting a new business was difficult, but soon after I got the business going, I realized that I thoroughly enjoyed the people contact and the satisfaction of helping people—something I had seldom experienced in my previous position in the construction industry. I learned that God knows me much better than I know myself.

Have you ever had an opportunity come along that requires making a crucial decision that could make or break you financially? Or how about a major life crisis that requires some serious thought to deal with it? I like how Eugene Peterson paraphrases Proverbs 3:5–6 in *The Message, "Trust God from the bottom of your heart; don't try to figure out everything on your own. Listen for God's voice in everything you do, everywhere you go; he's the one who will keep you on track."* As I have grown older, and hopefully wiser in my faith, I am learning the truth of this passage. God really does have a wonderful plan for my life. Unfortunately, too many times I don't wait to find out His plan. Instead I try to plow through on my own. And it's only when I get into trouble that I think that maybe I should check with God and His plan.

We seem to have a tendency to do things our way and then call on God when things don't work out quite as we expected. What a patient God we serve! Do you wonder if He tires of our persistent self-centredness, especially when all He wants to do is to bless us richly? His Word says that we should not worry about the mundane things in life, because if we seek Him first and His righteousness, all these things will be given to us.[24] In fact, Matthew chapter 6 begins by exhorting us to give and ends with telling us not to worry, that God wants to care for our needs. But isn't our attitude and practice concerning money the exact opposite? We begin by giving to ourselves and spend little time asking God how He would like us to use His resources—we don't seek Him first, and sometimes we don't seek Him at all.

I am an avid tennis player, and early on my instructor taught me about the sweet spot of the racquet. I find that when (the operative word here is *when*—I did say "avid," not "good") I hit the ball with the sweet spot or centre of the racquet, the ball responds better and is always more difficult for my opponent to return. In the same way, I have found that when I live "in the sweet spot" of God's plan for my life, things go much better and the devil has a much tougher time getting me off track. The key for me is to stay in the sweet spot. My attitude must reflect a trust in God to not only love me but also, because of that love, to know and want what is best for me.

---

[24] Matthew 6:33.

Kingdom Meditations

• Do you know what God's purpose is for your life?

• Are you spending time alone with Him each day to seek His plans for your life?

• Do your plans for today carry any recognition of His purpose?

• Do you think God is pleased with how you are using your time, talent, and treasure?

• When it comes to God's ownership, do you live like it's all His or mostly yours?

• If today the Lord asked you to show Him your bank statement and schedule, what would it say about your priorities?

• To what extent do you worry about things? To what extent do you try to control things?

• What would it take for you to experience contentment in the area of your finances?

• Spend time alone with God and ask Him to show you where you can add value to His Kingdom.

ENSLAVEMENT
To Debt

In 1989 an opportunity presented itself for me to leave my employment with the life insurance company and purchase a financial planning company. Doris and I began to lay this opportunity before the Lord. A little devotional book I was using directed me to look up a Scripture verse in Jeremiah. I did, but it seemed to have no connection with the devotional I had just read. It was then that I realized I had read the wrong passage. But I believe that the passage I read was the one God wanted me to see. It was Jeremiah 29:11, "'For I know the plans I have for you,' declares the LORD, 'plans to prosper you and not to harm you, plans to give you hope and a future.'" I felt God was speaking to me, and after prayer and seeking godly counsel I decided to leave my employer of twelve years and purchase an existing small business.

I will never forget the day we left the lawyer's office after completing the paperwork to buy this business. I said to Doris, "Well, how do you feel? We now owe more money that I ever thought I would make in a lifetime."

She was rather calm about it—as was I. You see, we believed that we had received direction from God to go ahead, and we trusted Him and His promise in Jeremiah 29:11.

So here I was with a corporate debt, the monthly payment of which was bigger than the entire mortgage on my first home. This thought made it easy to turn it all over to

God. I said, "God, this is Your business. I want to honour You with this business." Among other things, I promised God that if He would help me get out of debt, I would never again go into debt.

With God's help I set a course to grow this little company in order get the debt paid off as quickly as possible. When I was buying this company, there was a very small mutual funds business that was part of it and a reasonably profitable insurance agency. However, the mutual funds business had not made money in the three years it had been operational. So since it had never been profitable, I suggested to my accountant that we not buy the mutual funds dealership. He responded that the two seemed to go together, so why not? And so I purchased it along with the insurance agency. One year later the mutual funds business began to grow. It grew at an astronomical pace. Those were the best boom years ever in the mutual funds business. As it turned out, the portion of the business I was reluctant to purchase grew so fast, it paid off all of the debt within two and a half years.

And so we come to the issue of debt. The interesting thing about debt is that everyone seems to understand that it can quickly become your master, and no one wants to be under the bondage of debt, and yet statistics show that most Canadians are indeed not just in debt but deeply in debt.

We have become a nation that lives on debt. Proverbs 22:7 says, *"The rich rule over the poor, and the borrower is servant to the lender."* Throughout the Bible God speaks of debt as a curse. Often when the nation of Israel disobeyed in the area of finance, God would humble them by allowing them to get into debt. Deuteronomy 28:12 says that if we obey the Lord, He will *"open the heavens, the storehouse of his bounty, to send rain on your land in season and to bless all the work of your hands. You will lend to many nations but will borrow from none."*

Here are some current statistics on the state of debt in Canada:

• In 2003 Canadians paid 9.8 percent of our income on interest only on consumer debt while at the same time giving 2.3 percent to charity. That's 9.8 percent on interest only on consumer debt. And "consumer debt" does not include mortgages! That is really lifestyle spending.

• Near the end of the 1980s, the typical family saved just under 8 percent of its income. By the end of the 1990s, just ten years later, that same household spent one-tenth of a percent more than it earned.

• It was recently reported that 70 percent of families live paycheque to paycheque, making minimum payments on credit cards. Most Canadians have only two weeks money ahead.

• Bankruptcy rates are the highest in our history.

• In a poll conducted by Ipsos-Reid, 48 percent of respondents said they did not believe it was necessary to pay off all of their debts before retirement. Among working Canadians, 85 percent said it was important to escape their debts first, but one-third of retirees are carrying debt. The average debt load among retirees is $35,000, but 14 percent of them have debts in excess of $100,000.[25]

---

[25] I have used these statistics in various seminars and talks I have given over the last two years. I no longer have the exact references to give accurate credit, but I can tell you that for the most part they are taken from Crown Financial Ministries material and/or The Barna Research Group. I invite you to visit both of their Web sites to view this information for yourself: www.crown.org and www.crowncanada.ca and www.barna.org.

The culture we live in today trains us from the time we are young to live above our means to the point where we will be enslaved to debt our whole lives. I have heard it said that "We spend money we don't have, to buy things we don't need, to impress people we don't like." Maybe we need to stop viewing our lives in terms of what we lack and rather view them in light of what we already have.

I believe that our bank and credit card statements are theological documents that indicate the level of our obedience and our trust in God's provision. They tell who and what we worship. A friend of mine told me that while watching TV one night he added up what it would cost if he had bought everything that was advertised in two hours of watching. It added up to over $300,000. We are constantly bombarded with things to buy. And after we buy more things, and the novelty and short-term enjoyment wears off, we find that all we have is more things to look after. And so we look for something else to make us happy.

Here are some questions we should ask ourselves:

- Are money issues a strain on my marriage?
- Do I have overdue credit card debt?
- Do I carry a balance forward each month?
- Do I pay only the minimum payment on credit balances?
- Do I have at least three months of living expenses in a savings account?

Your answers to these questions may indicate that you are living a risky lifestyle. What happens if there is a job loss or any illness in your home? There is no flexibility.

Credit is too easy. Debt is at epidemic proportions. The reality that we are living in bondage to debt is easy to deny, even to ourselves. It's easy to live a lie and pretend we are something or someone we are not. After all, will anyone really know who owns it? Many Canadians are afraid to complete a net worth statement—some don't even know what that is. Your net worth is the difference between all the things of value that you own and all the debts you owe—in financial language, your assets minus your liabilities. Unfortunately for most, discovering their net worth may reveal just how desperate their situation is.

I received a call from a good Christian brother recently, asking me a very important question. The question was "If you knew that the market was to suffer a severe setback within the next three months, what counsel would you provide your family and your clients and friends?" The real question was "How should 'good stewards' be positioned in order to limit the fallout from such an occurrence?" I would continue to warn friends and clients about debt. A market crash is a good example of how those in debt can find themselves in dire straits in a heartbeat. In the event of a major turndown in the economy, many could lose their jobs and with large amounts of debt could then lose their homes, a catastrophic effect on families. But there are other world events that could place the debt ridden in great peril just as quickly—another 9/11, a major oil blip, an interest rate spike, or anything that can seriously impact the economy.

As Christians, we need to, as the Bible says, *"count the cost."*[26] It is important that each of us, at least annually, calculate our net worth or net liability as the case may be. We need to know. The Bible says, *"So if you have not been trustworthy in handling worldly wealth, who will trust you with true riches?"*[27] Have we been trustworthy? Would God think that we are being trustworthy if we have a negative net worth?

But here is something even more terrifying. One day we will stand before our Lord and Master, waiting to hear those words "Well done, good and faithful servant!" (Matthew 25:21), and we may not hear them. Why? Because everything

---

[26] Luke 14:28 (NKJV).

[27] Luke 16:11.

that He entrusted to us (in terms of worldly wealth) is now owed to someone else—everything. We are so far in debt that in essence we "robbed God."

Do you wonder, Christian friend, if we are losing our freedom? Are we serving money, or is it serving us? I know that if I hold anything too tightly, including money and possessions, then it probably has me, rather than me having it. Sometimes we can become enslaved to our money simply because we "think" that it's ours. Or sometimes, we become enslaved to it out of fear and insecurity—what happens if something unexpected happens, if I don't have enough money? How easy it is, as Christians, to say that we are trusting God with our eternal security and destiny but not our financial security. Viewed that way, it seems pretty silly, doesn't it? I have often heard people say, "It's only money." I wonder what would happen to this attitude if we changed the statement to say "It's only *His* money."

But there is more at stake here than money. We know that financial issues are the number-one cause of marital stress.[28] A recent survey I heard on the news said that Canadians worry more about money than they do about family members or any other thing. I believe debt is a "spiritual battle," and, therefore, debt will never allow us any freedom. Jesus says, *"No one can serve two masters. Either he will hate the one and love the other, or he will be devoted to the one and despise the other. You cannot serve both God and Money."*[29] We must daily choose whom we will serve.

Psalm 24:1 reminds us that *"The earth is the LORD's, and everything in it, the world and all who live in it."* The world may ask, "What does a man own?" but God asks, "How does he use what he's been given?" It's been said when it comes to wealth we are only poor if we want more than we have.

---

[28] Crown Financial Ministries statistics, www.crowncanada.ca.

[29] Matthew 6:24.

"So if you have not been trustworthy in handling worldly wealth, who will trust you with true riches?"[30] If we are in debt due to lifestyle spending, would God consider us faithful in the use of worldly wealth? Probably not. Jesus is teaching us that our faithfulness in worldly wealth leads to greater wealth in spiritual things. How can we lose if we are faithful in using the worldly wealth He gives? We win now, and we win eternally. Isn't that worth pursuing?

Let me say a quick word here about debt created by health or emergency issues. I believe that sometimes this type of debt is unavoidable. The debt I have been speaking to is not debt resulting from a large or unexpected health bill or some other major emergency that eats up all your assets. I pray that if you find yourself in such a situation that God will rescue you and that you find rest in Him.

Much of this book is the story of God teaching me His principles through my business life, but as I mentioned in the beginning, I am not always the easiest student to teach. Understanding these principles and faithfully applying them is sometimes a moving target. I find that I really need to continually look to God for His guidance in these matters. Allow me to share some things God has been showing me lately.

Every spending decision and saving decision has eternal significance. After all these years of serving Him, I think I am just beginning to understand this. When I grasp the significance of this statement, it really makes me pause and reflect on my use of His resources. Jesus told us not to lay or store up treasure on earth where it will be lost but to store up treasure in heaven where it grows for all eternity (Matthew 6:19–21). "Money invested in God's kingdom is immediately out of reach of the most turbulent of economic conditions. It is the most

---

[30] Luke 16:11.

secure of all investments."[31] So, I can spend the time and money God has given me on myself and my interests or I can be generous with it and use it to bless others. Notice I didn't say that I think God wants me to live like a hermit and give it all away. Nor do I think He asks you to do that. I do think that every buying decision should be looked at with this question in mind: Will this purchase help me to serve God better, will it help me draw nearer to Him, or will it draw me farther away?

I know I need to be more careful and prayerful about my spending habits. Recently I had need for a file cabinet for my home office. Doris and I checked out prices in many different stores and found they varied greatly. I told her I wanted to be a good steward of God's resources and didn't think that I needed a very fancy file cabinet. I chose the cheapest two-drawer black wooden file cabinet I could find, at about $30. When I went to pick it up, I found out that "some assembly was required" (don't you just love that?). It came in a very small box. I brought it home and began the hour-long task of creating a two-drawer file cabinet. It wasn't long until I found out why it was so cheap. As they say, "You get what you pay for." (Do you ever notice people only say that when you buy something cheap?) I now have a cabinet that in colour matches my desk but in quality is very poor. The drawers don't work very well; it has plastic handles and is made mostly of coloured pressboard. My reaction was, "Here I am trying to be a good steward and not buy the $100 model, and I end up with junk." As a good friend of mine says, "It seemed like a good idea at the time." In this case I would have been better off to have paid a little more and received quality that will last. This one is fine and will hold my files for now, but it won't last very long. Now understand here, folks, my intentions were very honourable. I thought that if I bought the cheaper one I would have more money to give away to God's work and God's people, in other words, "laying up treasure in heaven." As it turns out, I will

---

[31] Andy Stanley, *Fields of Gold,* Tyndale House Publishers, Wheaton, Illinois, 2004).

end up replacing that cabinet in short order and in the long run will pay much more—not a very good stewardship decision.

Buying decisions require a balanced outlook. I find that making the right choice is a fine balance and one with which I need God's help. A few months ago a good friend of mine was in need of a new car. His old one was often breaking down along the side of the road, and with winter coming on his wife was very nervous that it would happen in the cold of winter. He on the other hand thought that he would be a better steward if he could get one more year out of it. The Bible says one who fails to provide (look after) his own family is worse than an unbeliever.[32] I began to encourage my friend to get another car before winter. In this case, what appeared to be good stewardship was perhaps a bit foolish and maybe irresponsible. In the end my friend did buy a good second-hand car, paid cash, not taking on debt, and he and his family have been enjoying God's blessing and protection in a warm, sound method of transportation.

I want the things on which I spend money and time to be of benefit to others as well as to myself. A few months ago a friend of mine was interested in buying a cottage at a nearby lake. As a Christian he felt that he should get counsel from others before making a decision. When he approached me about it, the first question I asked was "Can you afford it, or do you have to go into debt to buy this second home?" He assured me that he could afford it and it would not put a strain on family finances. I then asked him why he wanted it. He said that he wanted a place for his family to come together. He felt that now that his children were grown and had kids of their own, if he had a cottage it would become a gathering place on weekends and holidays and a place to celebrate and enjoy times together. I thought that was solid thinking. I believe that God wants us to spend time with family and

---

[32] 1 Timothy 5:8.

friends and pour into their lives, and I believe that He is honoured in this way. I think God may allow us to have such places "for a season" so we can really spend some quality time interacting and passing on values and traditions.

Friends, when I see something advertised or displayed in a store that I sense an urge to buy, I ask myself, "How would I use this? Is it to bless and encourage others, or is it just for myself? Is it something I can use to connect better with my family or others in God's family? If so, how would I do that? And to whom am I accountable for following through on it so that I don't just use that thinking to rationalize the next purchase?" I find that when I spend money or time to acquire something that is just for me, it loses its attraction very quickly, but if I can press that purchase into service for others, that is when and where the real blessing begins.

While debt is not a good thing, neither is it always bad. I once heard a man say that "one should never borrow to buy coal." What he was really saying was that we shouldn't borrow to buy something that is used up or is a depreciating asset. I think that's good advice. So what about a mortgage on a house? Well, hopefully when we buy a house and borrow for a mortgage we have exchanged the liability of the mortgage we owe for an asset of equal or higher value, our house. The same holds true with a business. But what about borrowing to buy a car? Is it a depreciating asset? Some would question whether it's an asset or a liability, with all those repair costs, etc. Personally, I would prefer to pay cash, even if that means buying an older car. If you are not in a place where paying cash is an option, let me encourage you to take on as little debt as possible, pay it off as soon as possible, and then work to set aside some cash that can be used for this kind of purchase in the future. Just imagine what God can do with the extra money if we don't have to pay large interest payments.

In my twenty-five-plus years in the financial planning industry, I have learned a simple planning method. A good financial plan should help you deal with five things:

1) Recognize God's ownership
2) Spend less than you earn
3) Avoid the use of debt
4) Maintain three-months income for emergencies
5) Have long-term written financial goals and review annually.

Crown Financial Ministries provides good biblical information on creating a debt elimination plan.

Let me conclude this chapter on debt by saying that if you find yourself enslaved to debt and choose to do nothing about it, you will find the next chapter very difficult to embrace. Ken Boa puts an eternal perspective on our continually yearning for more "things" when he says, "Contentment is not found in having everything but in being satisfied with everything we have. The more we release temporal possessions, the more we can grasp eternal treasures."[33]

Kingdom Meditations

- Are you always striving for more than you have and living above your income?

- Do you know your net worth? Does that knowledge make you feel better or worse?

- How has debt negatively impacted your life? Your walk with God?

- What would it mean to you if you were debt-free? How would it impact your family life? Your spiritual life? Your giving?

- Are you ready to change your lifestyle to live a debt-free life pleasing to God?

---

[33] Kenneth Boa, *Conformed to His Image,* (Zondervan, 2001).

Contentment: *How Much Is Enough?*

After my first year in sales, I began my planning for year two and included a significant raise in income for myself. Each year-end thereafter for the next two years, I did a similar exercise, each time increasing my expected income, and each year I surpassed my goal. Praise God! It was at the end of year three that I sensed God saying to me, "Lorne, each year for the past three years, you said that if you could just make this much money you'd be happy, and here you are raising it again. *So how much is enough?*" Wow. I had not thought of it that way. I made the decision right then that I did indeed have enough and that I would be content. Now, I did not stop working; nor did I try to reduce my income. I simply stopped being "driven" for more and relaxed in what God had provided. Looking back now, I realize that as I became faithful to God's nudging, He was faithful in my continued increase. The difference was in my attitude.

First Timothy 6:6 says, *"Godliness with contentment is great gain." The Message* renders it this way: *"A devout life does bring wealth, but it's the rich simplicity of being yourself before God."* The NASB says, *"But godliness actually is a means of great gain when accompanied by contentment."* Now, you must agree that this a fascinating verse in Scripture, especially as we read it in context. This verse flows into the infamous and oftentimes misquoted verse that says *"the love of money is a root of all kinds of evil."*[34] We are told that those who seek to get rich fall into all kinds of temptation and ruin. The command to the man of God in verse 11 is to *"flee from these things...and pursue righteousness, godliness, faith, love, perseverance and gentleness"* (NASB).

I touched on contentment in previous chapters, but I think it needs further examination in light of God's call on our lives to care for His creation and all it contains, especially if it can sideline us, as these verses clearly suggest. What exactly is this thing called contentment? Did you know that the Old Testament talks about contentment 2,974 times and the New Testament refers to *contentment* or *sufficiency* 841 times? I don't think it is a stretch to then say that God wants us to be content.

If you will allow me to just ramble for a few minutes here, I'd like to share my thoughts in this area. I believe that a contented person believes that he has more than enough and actually feels blessed—that he doesn't deserve all that he has. A contented person is generous and sharing, because he often sees others who appear to be less fortunate and more needy than he. He has a sense of being blessed and wants to pass that blessing along to others. A contented person is a good steward of all God has given him. A contented person knows the answer to the question "How much is enough?" For John the Baptist, "enough" was an animal skin and sandals! It is said that a wealthy man is one who is content (in fact, that is the essence of 1 Timothy 6:6, isn't it?).

A contented person is transparent and real. He or she does not pretend or try to be someone they are not or live above their means. A contented person focuses on being the best he can be but not on how good others are or what they have. Contentment comes from living life "on purpose."

Contentment is an inside job. It's a decision we need to

---

[34] 1 Timothy 6:10.

make personally.[35] Have you ever met a contented person who wasn't happy? Or have you ever met a happy person who didn't live in contentment? I have not.

Contentment, once attained, can be lost easily. If we allow our minds to focus on the wrong things, it can be lost quickly. We need to discipline ourselves to be content and to focus on living as God would have us. To truly be content, as Christians we need to acknowledge that our future is in God's hands, and we can rest in the certainty that He always wants what is best for us.[36] I really believe that, don't you? All pain, discomfort, loss, and discouragement are only temporal and will pass.

The question is, how can we become content? So here are some things that I have learned. To be content I must:

- Ask God to align my wants and desires with His best for me.
- Stop comparing myself to others. God has made me unique.
- Spend time in God's Word and thank Him in prayer for His provision.
- Seek to discover the purpose, passion, and plans He has for me. (If you haven't set down and written out your personal purpose statement, then let me encourage you to do so before you go any further. It will help you be a more contented person in Christ.)

Are you still with me?—because this really is a crucial point that I believe God wants us to understand and live out. *"The*

---

[35] Psalm 84:10–12 is a good reminder. "Better is one day in your courts than a thousand elsewhere; I would rather be a doorkeeper in the house of my God than dwell in the tents of the wicked."

[36] Jeremiah 29:11.

one who received the seed that fell among the thorns is the man who hears the word, but the worries of this life and the deceitfulness of wealth choke it, making it [life] unfruitful."[37] *The Message* says, *"But weeds of worry and illusions about getting more and wanting everything under the sun strangle what was heard, and nothing comes of it."* Can you imagine running a race not knowing where the finish line is? How many of us go through life with no finish line when it comes to money and possessions? When asked the question "How much is enough?" John D. Rockefeller answered, "Just a little bit more." That, I believe, is what Jesus is talking about with the deceitfulness of wealth—always striving—striving for more because we never set a finish line.

When speaking to groups I am often asked, "Lorne, what is the answer to the question 'How much is enough'?" The answer is that it's different for everybody.

"Enough" is when we have enough to care for our needs.

"Enough" is not striving to raise our living standard year after year for its own sake.

"Enough" is not allowing our pursuit of possessions to distract us from our purpose in God.

"Enough" has forever dealt with pride slipping into our attitude about wealth.

And "Enough" continues to acknowledge our dependence on God to provide.

I heard a statistic that says if you have a combined household income in excess of $30,000, you are in the top 6 percent of this world's income earners. In Canada we are privileged beyond belief with the tremendous opportunities we have to build worldly wealth. I don't know the exact context, but Billy Graham has said, "If a person gets his attitude toward money straight, it will help straighten out almost every other area of

---

[37] Matthew 13:22.

his life." Wealth is not bad; in fact, the Bible views material possessions as good gifts from God, intended for our enjoyment.[38] It's the *love* of money that is a root of all kinds of evil.[39] Do we love money and possessions more than we love God? Which do we spend the most time thinking about?

God really does want us to be content. The lack of contentment in our lives can drive us to all kinds of problems, like covetousness, greed, envy, lust, and jealousy. All of these attitudes are ones Jesus expressly warned us against. Contentment is difficult to attain, as it seems it is our very nature to always want more. In our "flesh" we are never satisfied. And so the one who truly seeks to serve God and faithfully steward all that he has been entrusted with must answer the question "How much is enough?" Only then will he recognize the goal line.

And by the way, friends, I think that if you earnestly seek the answer to this question, the issue of the tithe will have taken care of itself. You see, tithing is an issue for many because the question is wrong. The question they are asking is "How much does God need?" Well, the answer to that one is simple—*nothing*—so anything you give above that is really good, right? So what would happen if, in your giving to God, you asked Him to help you answer the question "How much is enough for me?" and then ended that with the promise that everything above that will be given to Him and His work? We are asking God how much He needs, when we should be asking how much we really need.

One of my cousins was a missionary to Romania. While living there she met the man of her dreams and married him, a fine Romanian Christian. In the course of a conversation about his recent move to Boston with his new wife, he told me about his job and his understanding of the "How much is enough?" life question. He said that when he first went to

---

38 Psalm 81:9–16; Ecclesiastes 5:18–20; 1 Timothy 6:17.

39 1 Timothy 6:10.

work in the construction trade, he was paid $10 an hour. Shortly afterwards his boss gave him a raise. He said that he has continued to receive raises over this past year and is now earning $13 an hour. Now friends, here is where he is different from most of us living in this consumerist culture. He said, "I already know that we can live on $10 an hour because we have been living on it, so as the raises come in, I just give the rest away to God's work." Wow. Here is a man that knows how much enough is.

I am not suggesting that God wants everybody to live on $10 an hour. I don't think that God expects everybody to earn the same income. But I do think that we all need to know where the finish line is. I think in the game of life we need to know what race we are running.

How much income is enough for you? Let me encourage you to set a level of income that is enough for you and then tell God that you will give away everything He provides for you above this amount. Then watch what happens.

Kingdom Meditations

• What do you believe is the essence of godly contentment?

• Would those who know you characterize you as a contented person?

• Honestly ask yourself, "What am I striving for?" Make a list. Would God be happy with your list? Is it all for others or self?

• Ask God to show you what you are pursuing that is hindering true contentment.

• Can you answer the question "How much is enough?"

• How much is enough for retirement in order that you can be ready to volunteer your time and energy for God's purposes?

Learning to Trust HIM

THE FAST GROWTH OF THE COMPANY BALANCED PLANNING created all kinds of challenges. We worked very hard to ensure that we kept all of the promises we had made. Thanks to God's goodness, timing, and leading, I was able to pay off a ten-year mortgage on the business in two and a half years. God was teaching me that He will provide when I look to Him for the plan for my life and when I honour Him in the implementation. Remember, I had promised God that if He would help me pay this debt off early, I would never go into debt again. He was faithful in His part, and I have been faithful in mine. God is good. From that day forward I have never again gone into debt, for business or personal reasons. In those days in the industry, it was quite normal to see financial planning companies buying up other smaller companies. Many times other companies approached us, wanting us to buy them out, but as most would have required us going into debt again we never did. I decided that in order to live by the debt promise I had made to God, we needed to find a way to grow without incurring debt. The company grew from a small local business of 65 financial advisors to a national enterprise with over 1,200 advisors, and with God's help we did it all with no further debt.

In our Christian circles we often talk about the importance

of making Jesus our Saviour and Lord. And as I said earlier, I have found it is much easier to make Him Saviour than it is to make Him Lord. Accepting Him as Saviour is a one-time event; making Him my Lord requires daily intent and effort. And isn't it interesting that while we talk a lot about the importance of making Him Saviour, the New Testament refers to Jesus as Saviour only 25 times but refers to Him as Lord 600 times? That's quite a difference.

Is it possible that our problem making Him Lord is an issue of trust? Sure, we obey Him, but do we trust Him? After all, it is easier to obey God than to trust Him, isn't it? We obey because we believe it is the right thing to do. But to trust God requires that we believe in Him—believe that He will do exactly what He says He will do, no matter what. And that, my friends, requires not just faith but experience and a growing knowledge of God and His character—in a word, relationship.

Earlier in the book, I recounted my formative years, when I learned to obey God, when obedience was modelled for me. But I have had to grow into a relationship with God that would allow me to trust Him in all matters in my life, in particular the issue of money and the security of my future. The more I know God, the more I find Him to be faithful and the more I trust Him.

Recently I was meditating on Ephesians 2:10, *"For we are God's workmanship, created in Christ Jesus to do good works, which God prepared in advance for us to do."* I suddenly realized the impact of these words in my life. In 1946 (the year I was born), God knew that He would have some work for me to do with CNCF in the early part of the 21st century. So He chose for me to come into the world then and spend many years working in the financial services industry so that I would be seasoned and ready *"for such a time as this."*[40] That is a very humbling thought. It is my prayer that I will continue to walk in the way that He has prepared for me and will fulfill all that

---

[40] Esther 4:14.

He has planned for me in service to Him. I want to finish strong.

A friend of mine who spent many years in the real estate business trying to make a living confessed one day that many years earlier he had felt a call to full-time ministry, but because his dad had been a pastor most of his life, my friend said, "I can't live like that. My dad never had much; his income was so meagre." I watched this man work hard for years and years and then die, never having been truly happy. He also never made much money and always seemed to be going through tough times. His fear of financial insecurity never allowed him to reach out to the only one who could calm that fear. Job said, *"Though he slay me, yet will I trust in him: but I will maintain mine own ways before him."*[41] Trusting in God means that no matter what circumstances God may choose to allow in our life, He is still to be trusted.

My friend went through life trying to do it on his own, never trusting God and never experiencing the blessing that can only come when we are in the centre of God's will.

Andy Stanley says,

> In every person's life, God plants the question: "Do you trust Me?" To trust in Him financially means we experience peace and contentment while we enjoy the thrill of participating in His financial mission for the world...From my experience, I know it's a constant test of faith to live with an open hand financially, giving freely, and trusting God to replenish your stores of seed.[42]

---

41 Job 13:15 (NKJV).

42 Andy Stanley, *Fields of Gold* (Tyndale House Publishers, Wheaton, Illinois, 2004).

I have experienced what Andy is talking about first-hand. You see, after Doris and I sold the company (sorry, I'm ahead of the story here, but bear with me), we had enough money to live on. After our first year we decided that we should annually give to God's work an amount equal to our yearly expenses. Mathematically this doesn't make sense (or is it *cents?*). It should be pretty much impossible to get enough of a return on our investable assets to do this, but we are trusting God to make it happen. For five years now we been living on the return from our investable assets and have continued to give an amount equal to our living expenses for the year to the Lord's work at the same time. At present our assets are the same as when we started. I have never tried to figure out how this works, but I believe that by worldly standards it is impossible. But by God's multiplication, anything can work if we trust in Him.

Kingdom Meditations

• Reflect on what it means to make Jesus Lord of your life.

• In what areas of your life do you find it difficult to really trust God?

• Ask God to show you what do you need to do today to improve your relationship with Him.

• Reflect on your life to this point in time. Can you see God's hand working in you for such a time as this?

• Does the fear of financial insecurity hinder your ability to lead a full and abundant life?

Giving

Giving 10 percent of my gross pay when I was a salaried employee at the insurance company was relatively easy and required little effort or thought. However, as an owner of a growing and profitable corporation, it was not quite as simple. Did I tithe the before tax on the income of the corporation? The answer is yes—I did. And it was at this time that I began to raise the level of my giving well above 10 percent. What a privilege it was to realize that I was now able to give substantially more help to others! When all debt had been eliminated, I found it to be a real blessing to my family and personally uplifting to be able to give more generously. As I came to understand the truth of the statement "God owns it all," I started to think more about how God would want the other 90 percent used.

Many Bible teachers believe that learning to give is part of the maturing process—and that certainly has been the experience in my Christian walk. Until we have learned to give, we have not fully understood the gospel. We love because God loves us;[43] we forgive others because God has forgiven us;[44] we

---

[43] 1 John 4:10.

[44] Colossians 3:13.

welcome others because God has welcomed us; we accept one another because God has accepted us;[45] and we give because He has given to us (*"Freely you have received, freely give"*[46]). In this world we struggle and strive for worldly possessions; however, once we receive the gift of salvation, we realize that a man's life does not consist in the abundance of his possessions.[47] One aspect of loving one another is to meet the needs of another. Love is practical, not theoretical.

In the parable of the sheep and goats, we see that the Lord expects us to help our brothers who are hungry, thirsty, needing clothing, sick, or in prison.[48]

The believers in Corinth were instructed to set aside a sum of money each week in keeping with their income. This money was to help the poor Christians in Jerusalem.[49]

The story of the widow's mite shows that the condition of the heart is more important than the condition of the bank account.

> *And Jesus sat over against the treasury, and beheld how the people cast money into the treasury: and many that were rich cast in much. And there came a certain poor widow, and she threw in two mites, which make a farthing.*[50]

The mite was a bronze or copper coin so thin that it was called a "scale." It would take about four to make a penny. The message of Jesus is that God is not in need of money but of a humble, sacrificial spirit.

In the New Testament we find that giving to those in need is emphasized. When the Church was born at Pentecost, those

---

[45] Romans 15:7.
[46] Matthew 10:8.
[47] Luke 12:15.
[48] Matthew 25:31–36.
[49] 1 Corinthians 16:1–3.
[50] Mark 12:41–42 (KJV).

who had possessions sold them to provide for those in need.[51] As well, the early church measured their giving by the grace of the cross and not by the legalism of the Law, the early Christians did not limit themselves to the tithe. They gave much more. And they gave in the Spirit of Christ, as a demonstration of His pre-eminence in their lives, to help fulfill the Great Commission.[52]

When the Jews tithed by law, the poor usually went hungry. However, when the tabernacle was built with freewill offerings, people gave so much that Moses had to "pass a law" to stop it.[53] To make giving a legal act of worship causes people to look for legal ways to get around the "law." On the other hand, Christianity is a religion of the mind, heart, and spirit and should not be smothered by efforts to produce spirituality through external means.

In 2 Corinthians Paul talks about the grace of giving.[54] He makes the point that the gift is acceptable according to what one has, not according to what he does not have. He also makes the point that those who have plenty should help those who are needy, and, in turn, when we are needy they will be able to help us. The obvious point to make here is that the rich Western church should be contributing to the needs of the poorer church—we will be blessed spiritually.

The Bible is full of advice about giving to the poor.[55] One of the most efficient and effective ways I have found to give to the poor is through charities that run "microenterprise devel-

---

[51] Acts 2:45.

[52] Campus Crusade for Christ produces a wonderful self-study series on giving as part of their "10 Basic Steps Towards Christian Maturity," which can be found at www.10basicsteps.com.

[53] Exodus 36:5–7.

[54] 2 Corinthians 8.

[55] Matthew 19:21, Acts 9:36, and Acts 10:4 are just a few.

opment" projects. Several years ago, while speaking at a conference in Kuala Lumpur, Malaysia, I began wondering how I could make a difference in the lives of some of the poor in that country. It occurred to me that if we could somehow provide small loans to these people so that they could then buy equipment like a sewing machine to make clothes or other commodities, they could then sell those things to earn a living. I came back to Canada with the intent to start something that could accomplish that goal and assist other Christian believers who had a similar desire to reach out to the poor nations of this world.

Some time later I learned about a concept called "microenterprise development," which began as "microcredit"—the provision of small, collateral-free loans to the poor in developing nations. Over time, this term has expanded to include a broader range of services such as savings and insurance, all encompassed by the term "microfinance."

But poverty is multidimensional. Therefore, microenterprise development builds on the foundation of microfinance and adds business training, mentoring, evangelism, financial planning, and leadership development.

There are organizations that do this in a big way on behalf of Canadians. Two that come to mind are Opportunity International, Canada (OIC), (www.opportunity international.ca) and World Vision (www.worldvision.com).

A couple of years ago, Doris and I participated in an "Insight Trip" with Opportunity International (OIC). We went to Tegucigalpa, Honduras. There we witnessed first-hand the work of OIC and the microenterprise development program. We met one woman who received a loan for $300 to buy flour to make tortillas. Another received a loan for $450 to buy cornmeal grinders, and now she grinds cornmeal and sells it to her neighbours. These loans are repaid over a four-month period and reloaned out again to the same person or someone else who needs it. Many of these women told us that because of this loan program they are able to buy clothes for their family and send their children to school, which is critical to break the cycle of poverty.

By helping a poor family to increase their income, microenterprise development has an immediate and lasting impact on quality of life—the ability to afford food, shelter, education, and health care. As business income increases, the business is able to expand, and the effect spreads beyond the family into the local community, through employment and contribution to the local economy. Thus, the benefits of microenterprise development help grow not just businesses but stronger communities as well.[56] To me that is a genuine rendering of the principle of stewardship.

> *"Sell your possessions and give to the poor. Provide purses for yourselves that will not wear out, a treasure in heaven that will not be exhausted, where no thief comes near and no moth destroys. For where your treasure is, there you heart will be also."*[57]

When we understand the value of eternal things, we can let go of those temporal things we hold so precious.

The New Testament clearly affirms that God is interested in a love relationship with us. He wants us to enjoy His creation. God has shown Himself to be lavish in His grace and gifts. If He really is in us, then we will want to be like Him, and we are never more like Him than when we are generous.

First Timothy 6:18–19 says *real life* is attained when we give to others.[58] To me this is saying that being generous is what life is supposed to be about.

---

[56] This description of microenterprise is taken from the Opportunity International Web site: www.opportunity.org.

[57] Luke 12:33–34.

Isn't it amazing that He has chosen us to accomplish His work and that through this we can become more like Jesus? What a blessing!

[58] "Command them to do good, to be rich in good deeds, and to be generous and willing to share. In this way they will lay up treasure for themselves as a firm foundation for the coming age, so that they may take hold of the life that is truly life" (1 Timothy 6:18–19).

Kingdom Meditations

•Reflect on God's command to love others. What does that look like?

•How has God's message of giving to those in need in the New Testament Church affected how you live your life today?

•Do you give out of a sense of compulsion or a sense of freedom?

•Are you enjoying God's creation? Do you feel happy and content? If not, what do you need to do to fully experience God's desire for your life?

Saving and INVESTING

As Christians begin to respond to God's call to biblical stewardship, not everything becomes immediately clear. After the question about giving, probably the most common concerns arise around the financial principles of saving and investing—strangely enough, even before the issue of debt is resolved.

An often asked question is "Is saving for retirement biblical?" Good question! If we look to Scripture, we may not, at first glance see the answer clearly. Jesus tells this parable:

> *"The ground of a certain rich man produced a good crop. He thought to himself, 'What shall I do? I have no place to store my crops.' Then he said, 'This is what I'll do. I will tear down my barns and build bigger ones, and there I will store all my grain and my goods. And I'll say to myself, "You have plenty of good things laid up for many years. Take life easy; eat, drink, and be merry."' But God said to him, 'You fool! This very night your life will be demanded from you. Then who will get what you have prepared for yourself?' This is how it will be with anyone who stores up things for himself but is not rich toward God."*[59]

[59] Luke 12:16–21.

It sounds like Jesus is telling his disciples not to save up for retirement. Look what happened to this farmer when he decided to retire. God took his life. What did he do that was so bad? He had an extra good harvest—an extra good year in business, if you will. His income was so good that he could now retire. Is that so bad?

In Proverbs we are told that wise people store up for the future and foolish people use it all up now. *"In the house of the wise are stores of choice food and oil, but a foolish man devours all he has."*[60]

The same point is made elsewhere in Proverbs. *"You lazy fool, look at the ant. Watch it closely; let it teach you a thing or two. Nobody has to tell it what to do. All summer it stores up food; at harvest it stockpiles provisions."*[61] Once again God says that anyone who does not store up food is a fool.

The parable of Jesus and these passages seem contradictory at first, and since the proverbs are pretty clear, let's go back and look at that parable and see what Jesus is teaching.

This story is about a farmer who had an especially good crop; in fact, it was so good that he became rich with all his harvest. At the end of the harvest season the man sat back and said, *"Self, you've done well! You've got it made and can now retire. Take it easy and have the time of your life!"* (Luke 12:19 *The Message*). Then in verse 20 it says, *"Just then God showed up and said, "Fool! Tonight you die. And your barnful of goods—who gets it?"*

I have to confess, at first read, the farmer's actions don't seem bad enough to warrant death. In this parable we see a man who made an honest income and had a great year of earnings—in and of itself not a bad thing. The issue, I think, is selfishness. This man had an "I" problem.

He complimented himself by saying *I* have done well, and yet verse 16 clearly says *"The ground of a certain rich man pro-*

---

60 Proverbs 21:20.

61 Proverbs 6:6–7 (The Message).

duced a good crop." No credit given to God as provider. *"I've* got it made and can now retire." No thought of others; all he thought about was himself. He continues in this selfish pattern with *"I* will take it easy and have the time of *my* life." No thought given to how he might use the new-found freedom to serve God, since God provided the abundance leading to this freedom.

Then in verse 21 Jesus adds, *"This is how it will be with anyone who stores up things for himself but is not rich toward God." The Message* renders this verse as *"That's what happens when you fill your barn with Self and not with God."* Jesus is warning us about saving for the future without thought for His Kingdom—and the consequences are severe, to say the least.

So what about saving for retirement? Isn't that filling the barn for self? I think it depends on one's definition of retirement. Personally, I don't think I could retire and do nothing for very long, and, to be frank, I am not sure that this concept is part of God's plan for His servants. Just look at the ages of some of the heroes of the faith when God called them for His grand purposes. Abraham was 100 and his wife 90 when God fulfilled His promise of a son from whom a great nation would descend. Moses was 80 and Aaron was 83 when they were called to lead God's people out of Egypt. Surely if there was ever a case to be made for taking it a bit easier, these servants would qualify, and in fact each thought they were past the age that would make them effective for the task. But God's ways are not our ways. He had prepared them for this very time in their lives when they would make a significant contribution to His plan for His people. I have heard it said about Moses that he spent forty years thinking he was a somebody, forty years learning to be a nobody, and then forty years learning what God can do with a nobody.

As His servants, rather that being "retired," maybe we should call this phase of our lives "rewired." We are not retired; we are rewired for the next phase of God's plan for our lives. I know that in this phase of my life I want to use the financial freedom God has provided to serve Him by adding value to the lives of others, in whatever way He directs me. Henry Blackaby says,

> If you are God-centered, you will adjust your circumstances to what God wants to do. God has a right to interrupt your life. He is Lord. When you surrendered to Him as Lord, you gave Him the right to help Himself to your life anytime He wants.[62]

The verses in Luke 12 of the parable of the rich fool are prefaced by Jesus' words "*Watch out! Be on your guard against all kinds of greed;* ***a man's life does not consist in the abundance of his possessions***"[63] (emphasis mine). Here, I believe, is the real answer to saving for retirement. If what we have in RRSPs and other savings gives us a sense of trust or belief that our efforts alone will provide for our future, and if we fail to acknowledge that all comes from God and that He and He alone provides for us, then we need to heed Jesus' words in verse 15—to be on guard against all kinds of greed.

Now how about saving in general? Is it okay to save for future events, or should we just "let God provide"?

My understanding is that saving for a future event or retirement is in accordance with God's Word so long as we understand and appreciate that it is God's desire for us to have an abundant life,[64] free from worry about how we will live and

---

[62] Henry T. Blackaby and Claude V. King, *Experiencing God,* 15th Anniversary Edition (Broadman & Holman Publishers, 2004).

[63] Luke 12:15.

[64] John 10:10.

provide for ourselves and our families, and we are to trust Him to meet all of our needs and guide our living.[65] We go astray when we give in to the selfish motives that cause us to worry and fret about our future[66] and we lose sight of the fact that all belongs to God and we are His chosen caretakers. We spend a lot of time and energy worrying about what we don't have or won't have in the future. Sometimes I think if we spent as much time tending to what we already have, we would be much better stewards.

Investing

These principles apply in the area of investing as well. It can be a slippery slope to justify investing activity as our desire to be a "wise steward." Yes, God does call us to multiply what He has given to us. But He also cautions us about greed and wrong motives. Investing for the future is a good thing if our motives are in line with the Word of God. There is a difference between investing for a future event and hoarding.

A few years ago I was invited to invest in a project with some Christian brothers. This business opportunity was to provide us with a 20 percent annual return. It seemed like a solid opportunity with like-minded believers. In fact, the man running the business we were to invest in was also a good Christian man. I saw this as not only a chance to help this fellow get his business going so he could give more generously to God's work but also an opportunity for me to connect with other Christian businessmen in the city. Oh yes, the 20 percent return was certainly a factor.

I am sure you can guess the outcome and why I have included this story. A couple of years after my initial investment, the company went bankrupt, and I, along with the others, lost all of my investment. Shortly after this a good

---

[65] Proverbs 3:5–6.

[66] James 4:3.

friend of mine called to tell me about a "hot" stock he was buying. It had not yet gone public but would be doing so in the next year or two, and he felt that we could make a handsome profit if we got in then. I told him I would give it serious consideration.

After some prayerful time and thinking through the offer to "get in on the ground floor" of this new start-up company, I sensed God say to me, "Why would you choose to invest in this?"

"For quick gain," I thought.

Then God reminded me, "What does My Word say about quick gain?"

"Oh yes, God; it says that it's soon lost."[67] So I called my friend back and told him I would not be investing in this stock.

Friends, many times I hear Christian brothers and sisters talk about investing like it is a lottery—you put your money out there in the hope that you have the right combination and you'll come up a winner. It is also not uncommon that when asked why they invested in a particular area, Christians who invested poorly answer that a friend in their church sold them on it—an example of misplaced trust, to be sure. Why would we think that just because someone goes to our church or prays or reads the Bible at church that that alone makes them a good investor or advisor? We need to think about it, pray about it, and ask God to reveal our true motives. [68] Godly or greedy?

Some of you may have seen the film *The Corporation,* which explores the rise of the dominant institution of our time and its

---

[67] Proverbs 21:5.

[68] Crown Financial Ministries provides some excellent guidelines on investing on their website (www.crown.org) under Management Tools. I encourage you to examine your investing activities in light of God's Word.

grip on our lives. The film is based on the book *The Corporation: The Pathological Pursuit of Profit and Power* by Joel Bakan. The producers take the corporation's legal status as a "person" to its logical conclusion and ask the question "What kind of person is it?" The movie points out that the sole motivation of a corporation is to make profit for its shareholders—and as much as possible. The film goes on to show just what end some corporations will go to in their efforts to complete their mission. In one sequence we are introduced to a story about Terminator Seeds. In the name of profit, a corporation has developed seeds that are sterile after one crop, forcing farmers to buy seeds every year rather than save and replant. This ensures that the farmers remain dependant on the corporation, and the corporation is assured of future profits.

This got me thinking. Shouldn't we, as Christian investors and stewards of God's wealth, be asking the same question with respect to where we invest—What kind of person is this?

I believe that investing in the stock market is a good thing and, done with the right motives and proper advice, can be very fruitful for both the investor and the corporation into which he or she is investing. But I do think that God holds us to His high standard when it comes to multiplying what He has entrusted to us. This brings me to the subject of ethical investing or Socially Responsible Investing (SRI). I know it can be difficult when corporations are large and have diversified their investment over many different types of business, but I do think we need to have a greater awareness of the things we invest in and therefore promote. A buddy of mine who is a financial advisor tells me that in his practice he has actually seen churches with investments in pornography and other things that are totally counter to all that Christians stand for. I do not believe God will bless an investment in abortion clinics or pornography—and what about alcohol and tobacco, or companies that make weapons or destroy the ozone? I can't speak to how God will deal with each of us in this area, but I do think it behooves each of us to think about these things and make godly decisions.

Meritas Mutual Funds (www.meritas.ca) is one company I know that does a good job at helping investors keep "clean" on their investments. They are an SRI investment fund. They perform two levels of screening in an effort to satisfy concerns. First they do a "Negative Screening," which screens out companies involved in the production of tobacco and alcohol, military or weapons-related contracting, gambling, pornography, etc. The second level is called "Positive Screening" and is more proactive, selecting companies that show leadership in social issues, such as those with exemplary employee relations or companies that make a contribution to social, economic, or environmental sustainability.

However we choose to invest, let's remember that God owns everything, and He has chosen us to be His money managers.[69] Let's not fail to consult Him when we invest His money.

---

[69] Randy Alcorn has written a highly readable and short book called The Treasure Principle, Discovering the Secret of Joyful Giving (Sisters, Oregon: Multnomah Publisher). In it he outlines six treasure principle keys to truly experiencing joy in giving. The first is that God owns it all and I am His money manager. I encourage you to read this little book—it can be life changing.

Kingdom Meditations

• Do you have an "I" problem when it comes to your retirement planning?

• How does God's plan for your life factor into your planning?

• Examine your savings and investment history.

• Have you been guilty of hoarding? Talk to God and ask Him to renew a right spirit within you.

• Do your investments reflect your beliefs?

The WORKPLACE

AFTER I PURCHASED BALANCED PLANNING, MY ACCOUNTANT commented that most people going into a business never think about or make any arrangements to get out of the business. He encouraged me to not make that mistake. He said that it was wise when setting up a business to include an exit strategy. He suggested that because I was buying two separate companies, an insurance agency and a mutual funds dealership, for tax purposes upon eventual sale it would be prudent to have my wife own one company and me the other company. I agreed and instructed him to give ownership of the mutual funds company to my wife and the insurance company to me. I will admit that I was acting with my typical "male thinking" in doing it that way, giving myself ownership of the consistently profitable company and my wife ownership of the "money loser." So who says God doesn't have a sense of humour? You may remember that it was the mutual funds dealership that grew and profited quickly. So although my wife was not involved in the operation of the company at that time, it wasn't long before I was working for her, since it was her company that was by far the more profitable.

It was about this time when I read a book written by Larry Burkett called Business by the Book. (I recommend this book to everyone who is in a leadership role in business. CNCF now uses it as the textbook for a one-day seminar on how to run

> your business according to biblical principles.) I recall reading this book thinking, "Larry, you are carrying some things too far." And then I would search the Scriptures and realize that Larry was right. As a result of that study, I felt that I needed to bring a fresh understanding of integrity into my business.

The biblical account of Jesus' death on the cross says that at the moment of His death the curtain of the Jewish temple was torn from top to bottom.[70] From this point forward there is no hierarchy in service to God as there had been under the "law," where the Levites were the only ones who could serve God in His temple and where the curtain kept people from drawing near to the Holy Place. Now we are all His priests. And this means that we serve God every day, wherever we are, at work or at play. So, doing the work of God is now the job of every believer.

Now, some believe that work is a result of "the fall" and was never part of God's original plan. But in Genesis, Adam was to work in the garden to care for it,[71] so work is not the result of man's sin; it was just made more difficult.[72] So if work was ordained by God for man, then doesn't it make sense that God has a purpose for our work lives? Shouldn't we honour those purposes and glorify Him in our work? Friends, the enemy has misled us. How many times have you heard (or said) that your job is a necessary evil, a means to an end? The Bible says, "*We are God's workmanship, created in Christ Jesus to do good works, which God prepared in advance for us to do.*"[73] There is nothing in the verse to suggest that those "good works" are to be executed strictly within the confines of our church life. And yet, don't we all have a tendency to think that the work we do for God is confined to our ministry at our local church—and mostly on Sundays?

---

[70] Matthew 27:51; Mark 15:38; Luke 23:45.

[71] Genesis 2:15.

[72] Genesis 3:19.

[73] Ephesians 2:10.

When someone says to you that so and so has gone into full-time ministry, what do you immediately think? The pastorate—the mission field? Probably one of those two occupations, right? In the early Church, the believers spent most of their time in the marketplace, which they saw as both their business and their pulpit. They were in full-time business *and* full-time ministry.[74]

It seems that most Christians today are just trying to survive. Work oftentimes is nothing more than a route to a paycheque. We are not taking our faith into all parts of our life, and we are hardly even aware of this fact. Do we even hear the voice of God at work? Are we listening? Is there a relationship between our faith life and our work life? I have observed that those who separate their faith life from their work life oftentimes express a lack of purpose and meaning in their life in general.

Recently I heard Chuck Colson say, "Many are trying to build a personal Tower of Babel that testifies to their great skill and know-how. Yet when they stop building their careers and wealth long enough to take stock of their lives, they often find their lives are empty and their work lacks real meaning."

The buzz word these days in Christendom is *marketplace ministry.* The number of books being written on the subject and seminars and retreats taking place around the theme is voluminous. I am not going to attempt to add to the lot, except to say that it is clear that God is at work in the hearts and minds of His people about the integration of work life and spiritual life. At the back of this book, I recommend visiting the CNCF website (www.cncf.ca) for some great reading on the subject, and I encourage you to read some and ask God to reveal to you where you fit in His plans for marketplace ministry. I do however want to say that marketplace ministry is about more than sharing our faith in our sphere of influence.

---

[74] Ed Silvoso, *Anointed for Business* (Regal Books, 2002).

It is about acting with integrity in all that we do, using our skills and talents and power to make a difference in the lives of people, effecting real change in the world, to the honour and glory of God. Ken Boa speaks about biblical integrity this way:

> Biblical integrity is not just a matter of doing the right thing, it is a matter of having the right heart…the biblical virtue of integrity points to a consistency between what is inside and what is outside, between belief and behavior, between our words and our ways, our attitudes and our actions, our values and our practices.[75]

Just imagine if everyone who calls himself a believer lived in accordance with biblical principles, treated everyone they met with divine care, used the money and resources that they had been entrusted with according to God's purposes—would we recognize the world? Would there be the levels of corporate crime, poverty, war, famine, disease, violence in our homes—the list goes on—that we are witness to today? Would non-believers not be in awe of the way we live our lives? Would the name of Jesus not be spoken of with reverence?

Recently the Gallup Organization conducted a survey for the *Wall Street Journal* into the ethical behaviour of Americans in the workplace. The researchers found that there was no significant difference between churched and unchurched people when it comes to ethical behaviour and values on the job. What a disappointment! Where is the salt and light the Bible says we are to be in a dark world? Henry Blackaby writes, "You

---

[75] Kenneth Boa, *The Perfect Leader* (Victor, 2006).

cannot go with God and stay where you are."[76] I certainly believe this to be true in the business world. We need to be His hands, His feet, and His voice to all He puts in our path. Isn't it time we wowed our workmates and managers with our attitudes and servant hearts?

As I travel around the country conducting seminars based on Larry Burkett's book *Business by the Book,* there is one theme that I pray every Christian business owner hears through the prompting of the Holy Spirit, and it is this:

> *If we are ever to fully grasp how to operate a business on biblical principles and to integrate our faith and work, we must grasp the truth that God owns it all! We are His managers, His servants, His stewards.*

Now, what does that look like on Monday morning?

> People who are leaders first are too often those who naturally try to control, to make decisions, to give orders. They're "driven" to lead—they want to be in charge. And they're possessive about their leadership position—they think they own it. They don't like feedback, because they see it as threatening their position, the one thing they most want to hold on to.
> Leaders who are servants first assume leadership only if they see it as the best way they can serve. They're "called" to lead, rather than driven, because they naturally want to be helpful. They aren't possessive about their leadership position—they view it as an act of stewardship rather than ownership. If someone else on the

[76] Henry T. Blackaby and Claude V. King, *Experiencing God,* 15th Anniversary Edition (Broadman & Holman Publishers, 2004).

> scene is a better leader, they're willing to partner with that person or even step aside and find another role for themselves where they can better serve. They don't have the need to hold on to a leader's role or position if it doesn't make sense from the perspective of service.[77]

Over the years I believe that I have grown in my understanding of what God expects of me as a business leader, and some of that clearly has to do with decisions in financial matters. But God has shown me much more in the area of personal integrity and managing and leading people.

On the issue of integrity, one of the expressions that those who worked for us would have heard me say on many occasions was "If we just do what we say we are going to do, we will be well ahead of the competition." I really believe that, folks. If you do what you say you are going to do, you will set yourself apart. And with God's help, I try to practise it and lead with integrity in all things. When I fail, I need to recognize that and apologize to whoever is affected—irrespective of their job or status. Sometimes we as hard-driving type-A leaders feel the need to be right over the need to do the right thing. We mistakenly think we will be respected if we are right all the time—or at least perceived to be right. I cannot claim to have been perfect in this area, but I sure did try as God convicted me, and I believe I grew in my understanding and application. Allow me to share a couple of stories to illustrate.

I made it a point of company pride that our suppliers could say that no one paid their bills quicker than we did. Before I hired a chartered accountant as my controller, one day each week our payroll clerk would pay all the invoices for the week. Shortly after hiring this new accountant, I received

---

[77] Ken Blanchard, Bill Hybels, and Phil Hodge, *Leadership by the Book* (New York: William Morrow and Company Inc., 1999).

a call from a good supplier asking if we were having cash flow problems. The answer was no, and when I asked him what the basis for his question was, he informed me that recently we hadn't been paying our bills in a timely manner. My new controller explained that he was simply following standard accounting principles. I quickly explained our beliefs and practices, and from that point forward he complied with *our* standard principles. If someone supplied us with goods and services in a timely manner, we felt they deserved to be paid in a timely manner.[78]

I am proud to say that most of my business deals were sealed with a handshake (I can hear the "tsk, tsk, tsk" from all the lawyers). I will never forget a deal I made with a good friend of mine that required him to move from Eastern Ontario all the way to Vancouver, BC, to start a new work for us in Western Canada. When he made the commitment we had no contract—just my word. So I suggested that we draw up a one-page contract to protect him should I sell the parent company soon after his move. As it turned out, two years later I did sell the company. I let him know that I would be giving him a cheque as agreed and in accordance with that one-page contract. His lawyer, when informed about the conversation and the contract, told my friend that unfortunately that contract "was not worth the paper it was written on," the implication being that my friend would probably never see the money. So he was quite surprised when my friend later showed him the cheque for the agreed amount. The lawyer commented that he doesn't often see that kind of integrity.

The area of people management and servant leadership was something I had to grow into and regularly seek God's help and direction in. As a "driver" type personality and bottom-line thinker, the whole area of human resource management was a bit too "touchy-feely" for me. In fact, when we

---

[78] Matthew 7:12.

grew to a sufficient size that an independent consultant suggested that I needed an HR manager, I couldn't quite figure out what such a person would do.

But I did follow through and set up an HR department and in very short order began to see the vital role that HR can play in an organization. One of the lessons God taught me was that employees' personal problems did not stop at the front door of our office. Over the years, I had been ready to terminate employees based on things like consistent lateness, lack of work ethic (sometimes perceived, sometimes real), and many other very appropriate and justifiable reasons. Some of these people were Christians who I felt should be producing better and modelling good employee behaviour. I thank God that I had leaders who were close enough to the people and cared enough to be able to uncover some very ugly realities. Some of these employees were dealing with serious life issues, such as spousal illness, spousal abuse, and children on drugs and in trouble with the authorities. Instead of terminating them, we were able to take action that resulted in changed lives and circumstances: marriages healed, families given a second chance at wholeness, and many other situations. I believe God is honoured when we act out of love and care instead of expediency and economic interests. And the interesting thing is that the short-term cost and pain to come alongside these people and really lend a helping hand was more than compensated for by the goodwill this created and the employees who became very engaged in our success—those who benefited from our actions and those watching from a distance.

Another thing I learned was that by investing in our people, we invested in the business. For years I tried to get an employee suggestion program going, with very limited success. Then we implemented the "Killing the Sacred Cow" program. Without going into detail about the program, let me just say that this employee suggestion program was wildly successful, in part because it was innovative and fun but primarily because the program itself was created and executed by the employees, including the judging of the submissions. And we never ran out of suggestions; as a matter of fact, the list kept growing and the calibre of recommendations was extraordinary. This is what it means to empower your employees. Give them the authority and resources to impact their everyday work lives, and they will do more than you could ever imagine, and we will all win.

Somewhere along this journey we produced some Balanced Planning mugs as gifts—for our employees. Many companies have coffee mug giveaways for their clients, but we had these specifically designed for our employees. Along with our logo, printed on the mugs was the following:

> *Each person is a created being of infinite value and worth our time and commitment to help them develop to their full potential.*

Friends, this was not a ministry workplace (i.e., a church or parachurch organization), and most of our employees were not believers (in fact, there were only a handful of us). But by that point we, as a leadership team, were prepared to hold ourselves accountable to what we believed was God's truth and His calling to live out His commands.

I began to understand the awesome responsibility and incredible opportunity that leaders have to influence and impact people's lives by our actions and our care. I believe God was teaching me about relationship stewardship.

While we are on the subject of relationships, let me take few minutes here and again talk about debt—another type of debt many of us carry—relational debt. Romans 13:8 says *"Owe nothing to anyone except to love one another"* (NASB). I am afraid this is a debt many of us owe—in particular, we men. Oftentimes as business leaders we get into deep debt to our families. Relational debt, that is.

Over the years, God has clearly shown me the importance of relationships. After all, relationship with God is the primary difference between Christianity and other religions. God has shown us through the atoning work of His Son, Jesus, that He desires an intimate relationship with us. And through His Church He shows us the importance of spending time with God's people to encourage and support each other and His work. So I intellectually "get" the importance of relationships, in particular with my own family. However, there have been times when the workload has seemed so heavy that I felt that if I just put a bit more time into the business, getting it running a bit smoother, then I would be free to spend more time with my family. Sound familiar? The problem with this type of thinking is that "running a bit smoother" or "taking it to the next level" seldom happens, and even if it does, we are so busy we won't recognize it anyway. How many times have you said, "I can't help it right now, and anyway, the Lord knows my heart. He knows I would rather be with my family. I trust Him to look after them"? Isn't it interesting that we trust God to look after our families while we are away from them at work, but we never think to ask God to look after our work while we stay home with our families. We need to love our families, not just with our hearts but with our time as well. They can't see our hearts unless they are lived out in our schedules.

We owe it to one another to love and to show that love, especially to our own families. I am forever grateful to God that He did not lead me into business ownership until our children were in university and my wife was able to be my business partner. Many times when I had to work late, Doris was right there by my side. To those young families who may wish to start a business, let me caution you to pray and think carefully. Is this the time? God's Word reminds us that there is a time for everything.[79]

To determine if you are guilty of relationship debt, ask yourself some tough questions—and be honest in your answers.

---

[79] Ecclesiastes 3:1.

• Are you spending enough time with your children? Or are you just hoping they will turn out all right? Let me assure you, as one who now has adult children, that you only get one opportunity to influence them—and that time is now.
• What about your spouse? Does he or she get enough of your time?
• Do you participate in things that are of interest to your spouse or children?
• Are you building a relationship with your TV, hockey, or other sports or activity?

I find that my calendar can get filled up pretty quickly with "stuff," and none of it family stuff, unless I make family one of my top priorities. When we step across the tide of time into eternity, all that we take with us is our character and things we did for and with others. The Bible says in 1 Timothy 5:8 that if we fail to look after our own family we are worse than an unbeliever. And a word to those church leaders who may say, "Well my time is the Lord's, and I need to be about my Father's business." I do not believe that God ever calls us to violate one of His principles to accomplish His work. That's just not like Him. I have found this area of relational debt to be similar to financial debt in that it seems you just can't get ahead until you begin to get out from under the load, begin to pay back the debt and change behaviour. And if you think about it, the interest charge on relational debt grows much faster than on financial debt.

Let me encourage you to look at your schedule and determine how much time you are investing in relationships. And if you feel you are seriously in debt or in danger of being so, make a concerted effort to pay it off now. The consequences of not doing so are immense and eternal.

If we look at Jesus' ministry here on earth, we see that He spent most of His time in the marketplace, as do we. Of His

132 appearances in the NT, over 120 of them are in the marketplace, and almost all of His parables were built around marketplace examples. Now, here is a sad statistic I have heard: over 90 percent of Christians admit that they have never been trained to apply biblical principles in their work life.

I wish our pastors were better equipped to help us business men and women in this area. In all my years in leadership roles in my local church, I can never remember a pastor asking me how he or she could help me in my ministry at work. Most of my meetings with pastors resulted in them asking me how I could help at the local church. In fact, many of our church leaders and pastors likely know little about the business life of their parishioners.

Recently I heard about a pastor who not only makes a point of visiting his people at their places of work and praying with them but actually mentors a small group of businessmen in servant leadership principles. And mutual accountability and issues sharing is a regular part of their meetings. While I don't know this for a fact, I'm guessing that those men are growing in their Christian walk and bearing fruit for the Kingdom.

It is my hope that the disconnect between the church and our everyday work lives will soon be a thing of the past—that our seminaries and church leaders will begin to acknowledge that the real work of the church is to daily and weekly commission missionaries who will take the gospel into their workplaces (the marketplace) and influence others for Christ. I have found that freedom is not found in having and doing but in keeping God and His will first in my heart. Life becomes much more fulfilling and simple when I do the things that matter most. We need the encouragement and guidance from our spiritual leaders to keep us on the right path, doing the things that matter most for the Kingdom, and weeding out the "stuff."

To sum up, let me share with you some of the things I am learning in the area of the stewardship of my work life for God. I believe that we need to see all of our activity as God activity. We need an "all-the-time" awareness that God sees our every move and cares. On a daily basis and in particular when we are really busy, we need to ask ourselves, "Is this good activity or God activity?" As I go through my day I try to consciously say, "God, I know You are here. Help me to learn from You today and live in the sweet spot of Your will."

As a problem presents itself, say, "God, You knew about this since before time began, so let me turn it over to You. I need Your answer." Then be quiet and listen.

Many years ago when I worked for London Life we would often attend seminars, designed to teach leadership skills, given by Jack and Jerry Kinder, known as the Kinder Brothers. One of the sayings they frequently used to drive home the importance of leaders taking time to listen and reflect was "Don't just do something—sit there." That is still good advice today. Too many times as Christian leaders in business we get so busy just trying to "do something" that we don't take the time to wait on God to provide His answer.

Look for God in the little things. Look for Him in nature. Look for Him in the people you interact with throughout the day. Slow down. Take the slow lane to work in the morning. Park at the far end of the lot and walk to the building and talk to God about your day as you walk. Take the long checkout line at the store and pray for the people around you. It is amazing what God brings to my attention when I do these things. And this is not easy for a type-A personality.

The Message paraphrases Ephesians 2:10 as follows: *"He creates each of us by Christ Jesus to join him in the work he does, the good work he has gotten ready for us to do, work we had better be doing."* God has work for us to do for His Kingdom, and Sunday is the day of rest, not the one day we work for God. It is into the ordinary circumstances that God has placed us in that we bring honour and glory to His Name. Oswald Chambers says,

The test of a man's religious life and character is not what he does in the exceptional moments of life, but what he does in the ordinary times, when there is nothing tremendous or exciting on. The worth of a man is revealed in his attitude to ordinary things when he is not before the footlights (John 1:36).[80]

Psalm 139:1–6 (NLT) says,

O LORD, you have examined my heart and know everything about me. You know when I sit down or stand up. You know my every thought when far away. You chart the path ahead of me and tell me where to stop and rest. ***Every moment you know where I am.*** *You know what I am going to say even before I say it, LORD. You both precede and follow me. You place your hand of blessing on my head. Such knowledge is too wonderful for me, too great for me to know! (emphasis mine).*

---

[80] Oswald Chambers, *My Utmost for His Highest* (1935; reprint, Barbour and Company, Inc., 1963) Oct 12th.

Kingdom Meditations

- What is your definition of success?

- What is God's definition of success?

- In your work or business life, what can be seen that differentiates you from the non-believers next to you? Can your neighbours see a difference?

- Every day we preach to more people than our pastors do. Do we know what our lives and actions say about God's Kingdom?

- What are some steps you can take today to turn your everyday life into God's purpose?

SERVING
the Kingdom

Five years after I purchased the companies, I felt God again asking that very tough question, "How much is enough?" I began thinking back on the conversation I had with my accountant about the exit strategy. "When I plan to get out of this business, how much will I need to live on after the business is sold?" So during the summer of 1995 I hired a consultant to assist Doris and me with the answer to that question. At the end of that exercise and after much prayerful thought and counsel, we came up with a number. We felt that with this number invested conservatively, we could comfortably live off the earnings.

It is interesting that we had dealt with this question in 1995 because in 1997 I sold both companies to a public consolidator for much more than I had ever anticipated they would be worth. I am grateful that God prompted us to set our income level two years earlier when I didn't know what the company was worth. Otherwise I might have tried to rationalize why I needed to keep more of the money for my own enjoyment. When the sale was complete, we didn't have a decision to make about how much we should keep for ourselves and how much we should give away. The sale made it possible for me to enjoy the privilege of volunteering my time to CNCF, and our income decision has allowed us to experience the joy of giving to many projects.

The sale closed in April of 1997. As one might expect, with a sale of this kind, the larger portion of the payout was in the form of stock of the purchasing public company. So now I had God's money from the sale, and I wanted to be a wise steward for Him. I did not think it would be wise to give too much to any one charity all in one year. It could ruin a small charity if they received a large gift all in one year. But as always, God's timing is perfect. At that time Revenue Canada changed the tax laws to allow for a significantly greater tax benefit to a donor giving public stock to a public foundation than if that same donor gave cash. So because of the tax benefit of giving appreciated stock over cash, I wanted to give stock. I had until December to decide to whom and at what level I would give. But God was in control.

That same year, a close friend of mine also had a large gain on public stock and, to benefit from the tax deductibility, needed to give it away in that calendar year. So the two of us went to a mutual Christian friend who is a lawyer and asked him to help us set up a public foundation. We soon learned that to be considered public we needed to be sure that no one person ever contributed more than 50 percent of the assets in the foundation. We were able to give this appreciated stock to a newly formed foundation, which today is known as the Canadian National Christian Foundation (CNCF). In return we received a donation tax credit and preferential tax treatment on the related capital gain to realize substantial tax savings. Once the assets donated had been sold by the foundation board and turned into cash, we were able to advise the board as to which charities to give to and in what amounts.[81] It was like having a family foundation without the costs and hassles of ongoing tax and management of the assets.[82]

---

[81] Some charities may not have the inclination or the infrastructure to convert assets to cash and may find a public foundation helpful in this regard.

After the sale I agreed to stay on as CEO of the company and lead it through a transition time. I left the company and the business world five years later for what is commonly called retirement. As I said earlier, I don't like to think of myself as retired so much as rewired—rewired for the next phase of God's plan for my life. I was ready to get on with something new for my Lord.

At first I thought it would be great to lead and influence another company in a new location. And because I had already answered the "How much is enough?" question, I knew that I was not looking to earn a large income. But I did think that I could provide a Christian influence in a new company somewhere else. This seemed like a noble cause—having "influence for the Lord" in another secular environment. I told the Lord that if He would give me the leadership role in a new company, I would give 90 percent of what I earned to His Kingdom.

Not long after I received a call from a very successful businessman in Toronto, who asked if I would do some consulting with his company as they were going through some changes. This company was similar to the one I had just sold. I thought this could be fun and I could have a godly influence. Well, I wasn't long in this role of consulting and giving away 90 percent of what I earned before I discovered that this wasn't as much fun as I had first thought. *God showed me my real motives.*

God showed me that my initial motives certainly seemed pure—desiring to influence others for Christ—but what was really driving me was the fear that I would have no income other than the earnings from the assets He had already provided. It was scary to think that no more cheques would be coming in. God helped me to realize that selfish-

---

[82] Early in 2006, the government enhanced the benefit of stock donations to public foundations and charities even further. Now when giving appreciated publicly traded stock, there is no taxable gain on the gift. For more information on this, please discuss with your accountant or financial advisor or contact CNCF at www.cncf.ca.

ness and fear were driving me. I still wanted to be in control of the income.

I took the next year seeking God's direction. I prayed, read the Bible and other books, and sought counsel from Christian brothers. As a "just do it" kind of guy, it was difficult to simply sit and wait on the Lord. God's timing is definitely not my timing. He often takes significantly longer to show me His plan than I would prefer. Maybe it's because I have poor "spiritual eyesight," or maybe it takes Him that long to get me prepared. But of course in hindsight, His timing is always perfect. I am slowly learning to be patient and not rush ahead of God. And I am sure that God is not yet finished with my education in this area.

And so I waited on God to show me the next chapter. I began to hear a common message from other Christians, that God wanted me to give leadership to this new foundation—a national public foundation that would serve the needs of the Canadian Christian community. I must say that I didn't immediately embrace the idea. I envisioned myself sitting in an office somewhere waiting for donors to pass assets through this foundation to the charity of their choice. It sounded pretty boring for a "let's just get on with it" kind of person like me. But what I really needed to know from God was whether this was what He wanted me to do.

I did indeed then get a strong sense that God wanted me to give leadership to this start-up foundation. I wanted to know for how long. I sensed God saying, "I want you to put your head down and give this foundation your full attention for the next two years."

I have heard it said that if you want to know God's will for your life, it works like this: If I invited you over to my house for dinner tonight, I could send you directions via e-mail or I could give you directions over the phone. But with either of these methods it would be easy to create a misunderstanding and you could get lost. However, I could get in the car and ride with you. If I did that I would say, "Go down this street and turn right at the third light." Then I would not give you any further directions until we had made the turn at the third light. Then

I would tell you the next turn. I think that sometimes that's the way God gives us direction in our lives. I am learning that if I don't put the car in gear and just sit in the driveway and roar the engine, God has no reason to give me further direction. If I haven't acted on what I already believe to be His instructions, why should He give me any more direction?

So here I am, already past the "next two years" and excited by what God is doing with this foundation. I needn't have worried about being bored, because what God had in mind for the role of the foundation is not only more original that anything I could have thought up, but He has called, and continues to call, others with exactly the unique gifts needed to strengthen the team and join together in serving the Kingdom.

Thank you for persevering through my story and my musings. You are to be congratulated for "hanging in" and granting me grace where you might have disagreed with my thoughts.

As I said at the beginning of this book, this is my story of how God has dealt and continues to deal with my little kingdom of self and has helped me to begin to dismantle walls so that I might experience the joy of being a generous giver and live a life that I hope will be pleasing to my Lord and Master. And as you have seen, many of the lessons learned have to do with money and possessions. But one of things I have learned along this journey is that my handling of and attitude towards money and possessions is oftentimes used by God to show me His heart and to teach me His ways. God's will for me (and for you) is to be conformed to the image of His son, Jesus. And to that end, He is looking for His servants to choose service to Him over self-interest.

In the book, *Follow Me*, the author speculates about what God could do on this planet if those who claim to be His would exchange keys with Him. And by this he means, God "gets the keys to my kingdom treasures and I get His keys to His kingdom treasures. If the total resources of evangelical Christians were released under the direction of the Holy Spirit, every worthy ministry objective could be adequately funded with a surplus left over. The world could be radically influenced as Christians exchanged treasure with God... When the people of God are aflame with His kingdom, their lives burn with generosity and magnanimous sharing but are never depleted... Christian love keeps flowing out with a generosity motivated and resourced by the Spirit of God."[83] How attractive would that be to a hurting world who does not yet know the love of the Father?

Let me conclude by posing a few questions, ones that I try to keep before me at all times.

Am I an owner or a manager? Continuously in my Christian walk, I must deal with this question – because one thing I do know for certain, I am not taking anything other than my character and my spirit with me when I depart this world. And God's Word makes it crystal clear that He will hold me accountable for how I manage what He has given me.

Whose kingdom am I building – mine or God's? Moses was 80 years old when God called him to his life's work and God's Kingdom purposes. Everything that happened to Moses up to that point was part of God's plan for his life. Am I building God's Kingdom now where He has placed me? Or am I busy climbing the ladder of success only to find out one day that it is leaning against the wrong building?

Am I experiencing the abundant life Jesus promised He had come to give?[84] Is the burden of debt or a heart of discontent robbing me of the abundant life? Do wealth and possessions have a hold on me in conflict with my Kingdom values?

Is my heart fully surrendered to God? Does my life and everything in it truly belong to God? Have I placed all at His disposal?

---

[83] Jan David Hettinga, *Follow Me* (Colorado Springs, Colarado, Nav Press, 1996) pg. 252.

[84] John 10:10

Does my worship involve continually transferring all that I have to the Master?[85] God has given us very specific instructions about the use of His creation and everything in it. How many of us will be handing God an IOU when we stand before Him longing to hear those words "well done, good and faithful servant... come and share your master's happiness"?[86]

When we truly embrace stewardship as the call of God on our lives, we will together change the world and the Kingdom of Heaven will have come. As the Bible clearly says: *The time is fulfilled, and the kingdom of God is at hand.* **Mark 1:15.**

My pledge to you is that you will be in my prayers daily. I may not know you by name, but as this book makes its way into the places chosen by God, my prayer will be that God's intended message will be written on the hearts of those who read it and that He will use my story for His purposes.

---

[85] Jan David Hettinga, *Follow Me* (Colorado Springs, Colarado, Nav Press, 1996) pg.

[86] Matthew 25:21.

Appendix A

THE FAITH DECISION

FRIENDS, SOME YOU READING THIS BOOK MAY FIND THESE phrases a bit unusual and uncommon and maybe even uncomfortable. You may even be saying to yourself, "Okay, not words I would use, but I get it. I try to live the kind of life Lorne is talking about and, for the most part, do a fair job. And I do believe there is a God. I am not quite as intense as Lorne is about the whole thing, but I get it." If that is your thinking and you really would like to understand this whole faith and salvation thing a bit better, I invite you to visit any of the Web sites listed below that explain the Christian message of salvation through Christ in very clear and understandable language.

The following is my rendering of the message of God's wonderful plan, the good news of salvation—in other words, the gospel message. It is a compilation of the explanations used by The Navigators, Campus Crusade for Christ, and the Billy Graham Evangelical Association.

God's Love

God created us in His own image to be His friend and to experience a full life assured of His love. But He didn't make us robots—He gave us the freedom of choice.

The Bible says,

> *For God so loved the world that he gave his one and only Son, that whoever believes in him shall not perish but have eternal life"* (John 3:16). Jesus says, *I have come that they may have life, and have it to the full* (John 10:10).

Our Problem

All of us have done, said, or thought things that are wrong. This is called sin, and our sins have separated us from God. This separation means the penalty of an eternal spiritual death.

The Bible says, *"All have sinned and fall short of the glory of God"* (Romans 3:23). God is perfect and holy, and our sins separate us from God forever. The Bible says, *"The wages of sin is death"* (Romans 6:23).

God's Remedy

On our own, we cannot attain the perfection needed to bridge the gap between mankind and God. Therefore, God has taken the initiative to restore us to a right relationship with Him. He sent His only son, Jesus Christ, to die for our sins. Christ's death alone is adequate for our sin and bridges the gulf between God and man.

Jesus is the Son of God. He lived a sinless life and then died on the cross to pay the penalty for our sins. *"God demonstrates his own love for us in this: While we were still sinners, Christ died for us"* (Romans 5:8).

Jesus rose from the dead, and now He lives in heaven with God His Father. He offers us the gift of eternal life—of living forever with Him in heaven—if we accept Him as our Lord and Saviour. Jesus said, *"I am the way and the truth and the life. No one comes to the Father except through me"* (John 14:6).

God reaches out in love to you and wants you to be His child. *"As many as received Him, to them He gave the right to become children of God, even to those who believe in His name"* (John 1:12 NASB). You can choose to ask Jesus Christ to forgive your sins and come into your life as your Lord and Saviour.

Our Response

Believing means trust and commitment—acknowledging our sinfulness, trusting Christ's forgiveness, and letting Him control our life. Eternal life is a gift for us to receive.

If you want to accept Christ, you can ask Him to be your Saviour and Lord by praying a prayer like this:

> *"Lord Jesus, I believe You are the Son of God. Thank You for dying on the cross for my sins. Please forgive my sins and give me the gift of eternal life. I ask You into my life and heart to be my Lord and Saviour. I want to serve You always."*

http://www.billygraham.org/SH_StepsToPeace.asp
http://www.navigators.org/us/resources/illustrations/items/bridge
http://www.4stepstogod.com/

Appendix B Helpful Resources

The Serving the Kingdom Partnership is a concept developed by the founders and leaders of The Canadian National Christian Foundation (CNCF), who understand that stewardship is about more than just the management of money; it is a working out of the call to serve God with all that we are and all that He has given us.

We work with givers to connect God's money with God's work. We work with financial professionals to help integrate biblical principles into the practical financial advice they provide their clients. We invest in leaders of churches, charities, and ministries, helping them to connect and maximize their efforts, making good use of the resources entrusted to them.

We believe that God is calling us to encourage, empower, and equip believers towards a better understanding and living out of Christ-centred stewardship.

For up-to-date materials that can help you to fully embrace your role as God's steward, visit any of our websites at

- www.servingthekingdom.com
- www.cncf.ca
- www.advisorswithpurpose.com

and click on the Downloads icon. There you will find a recommended list of reading material and names of organizations and Web sites that can provide practical guidelines for things like debt elimination, biblical investing, biblical principles for business owners, and much more.